dog-ma

the zen of slobber

barbara boswell brunner

My four-legged friends…
May your angels all fly free.

Kashi	Black Doberman	1980 – 1996
Turbo	Blue Doberman	1986 – 1993
Lexington	German Rottweiler	1993 – 2002
Madison	Black Lab/Dalmatian	1995 – 2010
Gus	Brittany Spaniel	1993 – 2008
Sutton	American Rottweiler	1997 – 2004
Cooper	Red Doberman	2003 – 2011
Morgan	German Rottweiler	2004 –
Izzy	Parson Russell Terrier	2007 –

"Animals do have a voice. If you ignore their suffering, I will remind you of it. If you don't understand them, I will translate. If you don't hear them, I will be their voice. You may silence them but you cannot silence me as long as I live."

~ Anita Mahdessian

ACKNOWLEDGMENTS

Writing Dog-Ma has been a sixteen-year process, beginning just in my head after the loss of our first dog, Kashi. Ink to paper only followed after many years of encouragement from family and friends. Retirement afforded me the time to begin the long process of organizing my thoughts into what I hope is a humorous yet poignant story of the animals that have touched my life. Family and friends have added their own personal accounts to each chapter, offering many stories I had long forgotten. My thanks go out to everyone who has helped me along the way.

Ellen Jordis Lewis, you have been my inspiration and coach. Without your constant support and re-writes, my manuscript would have been tossed into a dusty drawer long ago. The cover and artwork could never have been as amazing without the artistic skills of our dear friend Dane Johnson. Michael and Lisa Williams, Karen McClain, Kristin Brunner, Matt Wilkerson, Dow O'Neal, Carol Franksen, Sally and Joe Beynon, Kim and Richard Caputo; the stories you refreshed in my thoughts will be cherished. Jessica Franksen, your photos of the dogs will be my forever treasure. Thank you for allowing me the opportunity to use a few for this book. To my father, Robert Boswell, thank you for instilling in me, at a very young age, a love of all animals. Nanette Weaver, editor extraordinaire, I thank you for reminding me of my significant overuse of OK, Ok, okay. Finally, thank you to my fabulous husband Ray without whom none of this story would be possible. Thank you for your support and patience when I said "Wait, just give me one more minute to work...no really, just one more minute..."

Cover Design – Dane Johnson Design
Cover Photography – Ray Brunner
Interior illustrations are inspired
by photography from – Ray Brunner,
Barbara Brunner and Jessica Franksen

Blood

It is everywhere. The stark white walls shimmer with droplets like a Jackson Pollock painting. My hand pulses with pain as I struggle to separate the combatants, one collar in each outstretched hand. Rivulets of red run down my arm and I am unsure if it belongs to me. I cannot, I must not fixate on it. My heart pounds until I am sure it will escape my chest; each beat pronounced and strong. My predicament is clear: let go of one and the other will perish. I must hang on and wait for calm to prevail. Breathe deeply. Show control. No, TAKE control. I try convincing myself this will all be over soon. I cannot scream; it would only exacerbate their fury.

Time slows as though the clocks have momentarily stopped. With each breath, the pain of my hand surges through my body. Morgan shakes her head and dots of red splatter onto the floor. The soft white fur surrounding Izzy's mouth is stained with a cocktail of gore. Her blue-clouded eyes sparkle as she gazes blankly in an undetermined direction. She cannot see her intended adversary, having been robbed of vision a year earlier. Her snarls are guided by her nose; her anger guided by fear.

As my muscles strain to maintain the distance between the combatants, I hope for a reprieve. I struggle to control one hundred and twenty pounds in one hand and twenty pounds in the other, tenacity compensating for the smaller stature. Deep claret tones slowly ooze through her long white, wiry fur. I can already see her eye beginning to swell shut, like a prize-fighter on a losing day. Morgan is dripping blood. Izzy's tooth has ripped a gash in the tender velvety lining of her ear. She shakes her head to ease the pain. If I wasn't so damned pissed off I could appreciate the artistry of the spatter, with flow and movement as intricate as any piece of MOMA artwork.

"Leave it!" booms from around the corner. Ray extricates Izzy from my hand, gently coaxing her to settle down. Izzy's maniacal temper has not eased, evidenced by her continued struggle for freedom.

Izzy has only one mission: kill or be killed. It does not matter that the Rottweiler is six times larger or has jaws that could crush bone. She must prevail. Failure is not an option. She is a terrier.

Ray has a soothing effect. Izzy feels safe in her human dad's arms.

They have much in common: determination, stubbornness and moxie: two peas in a pod. Where they differ is in temper. Izzy has no control over hers. When the anger switch flips in her tiny little brain, no one can turn it off. She is focused to a fault, her tantrums often triggered by the fear of her sightless world.

Morgan sighs. She is ready to be released. She quiets easily and quickly. She is a gentle giant, not a fighter. She bites only to defend herself. If her intent were to eliminate her assailant, it would happen in one quick snap of her jaw. She cannot understand why this monster was brought into our peaceful home. We were a happy family until Izzy appeared. She is the Anti-Christ. She is pure evil. Our home has become a salient battleground with opponents always vigilant, wary of the other, waiting for the first sign of war.

Finally, the opponents are separated, sent to their respective corners. Equanimity has settled in, not like a comforting blanket, but a static-filled one; on edge and ready to snap at the first sign of friction. I wonder how our family became ensnared in this violence. It wasn't always this way.

There was a time when our home was a sanctuary of Zen-like calm, a respite from our hectic professional world. We rescued abused and abandoned animals, provided them with comforting shelter and loving care. Yet, here I sit on the kitchen floor, assessing the multitude of damage, wondering where we failed.

This is where it begins:

Hover Baby, Hover...

Serenity and beauty. Good goals to strive to attain throughout life, don't you agree? I remember thinking this, even as a child. I always changed into a clean dress to go to the grocery store with my mom. I didn't like to play in the mud and get dirty. I enjoyed being clean, pretty and girly. While my tom-boy sister played in tee shirts and shorts, I always preferred a dress. Ribbons in my unruly curly hair— definitely! Early in life I trained as a competitive figure skater. I loved the surge of power and energy of jumps and spins, then carving tiny lines into the ice to make beautiful patterns. Chaos, calm, crisis, centering. Somehow, the contrast felt right to me.

Decades later, I fell in love with a man who shared my passion for beautiful environments. I dedicated my professional life to helping people relax and be at peace through several retail stores I founded. Whether my customers needed soothing sea salts for their bath, a beautiful piece of jewelry or new yoga attire, they came to me to seek relief from their own hectic world. I named my company Urbane Zen, a fitting name for a sophisticated, peaceful environment. The sparkling centerpiece of each of my stores was a jewel-colored soap bar showing fifty gem-like varieties, each handcrafted from the finest natural ingredients. Quiet soundtracks played in the background. As soon as the door to Urbane Zen closed behind you, the traffic and stress of the outside melted away.

Now open the door to my home, to the slobbering, teething, shedding, barking, jumping, vomiting mess of nine Godzilla-size dogs. To be accurate, only eight were actually physically gargantuan. Our latest addition, at twenty pounds, is enormous only in spirit.

Our home is in a constant state of chaos. The dogs' behavior...mortifying on every level, but I never apologize. An invitation to our home comes with a caveat. "Hi, welcome to my home," with the unstated message, "where you will be crotch-poked, butt-sniffed, licked endlessly and returned to your own home covered in assorted shades of dog fur, smelling like a kennel." Oh, and did I mention, you must guard your dinner plate like a tenth-grader taking a test next to the cheating football player? Hover baby, hover.

It's all about balance.

Retail Vagabonds

Ray and I met in the late 1970's in Washington, DC, both having been transferred into the DC area by our company, The Gap. Yes, yes, yes...the clothing company now called GAP. For those who are less than ancient, GAP dropped "the" in the early 1990's to sound more hip, which makes all of those iconic "Fall Into The Gap" commercials so useless but still hilarious. Our first contact was a Regional meeting where I was seated with my best friend at a table in the back of the room. From this strategic location we could cause generalized chaos and not get noticed flirting with the new curly-haired, beach-boy looking guy. Suddenly the new guy catapults himself across several tables to land in the empty seat beside me. "Hi, my name is Ray." This high-jumping Phenom was my new boss's boss. Uh oh...trouble was brewing...

Ray and I were drawn together by our love of dogs. I grew up in a houseful of terriers, Welsh and Wirehaired Fox to be exact. We also had a one- year-old German

Shorthair that my dad rescued. Greta was so badly behaved that after just five days my mother threatened to move to a hotel until the dog found a new home. Greta must have been put into the witness protection program because she was gone by nightfall. Mom had POWER!

Ray grew up with beagles. Each of their dogs was always named Guess. Ray and his dad had a great sense of humor and always thought it was funny when people would ask the name of their dog and their answer would be "Guess." The inevitable question came back and again they would reply, "Guess." They got a lot of mileage out of that bit of twisted humor.

Despite his mother's dislike of dirty, stinky, shedding animals in the house, Ray and his father would sneak the dog in when she went out to shop, always resulting in a good scolding later in the day. Ray and his father both shared a common gene, one that imparts the inability to notice that a dog can shed a huge mound of fur on the floor, plod through the kitchen with muddy feet and knock over the trashcan to scavenge for treasure. It's a gift...truly...a gift.

Ray's dad Paul was a huge animal lover. He loved them all and they loved him back. He seemed to communicate with them on a different level. Years later, our Dobermans had him wrapped around their giant paws. He spoiled them worse than grandchildren, sneaking them food even though he knew they were never allowed people food. Paul and Ray's mom, Irene, house sat for us during one of our home relocations. We left them with a dog weighing one hundred pounds and returned to a dog weighing one hundred-*thirty* pounds. In a month! Apparently they shared a passion for hot dogs and ice cream.

Dog-sitting Ray's dog, Brandy, evolved into dating and soon we were inseparable. I resigned from my job (yes, I found a new one, thank you) and Ray received the first of many, many job transfers. As we began our gallivanting life of retail vagabonds, Brandy stayed behind with Ray's daughter, Kristin, who was ten years old and an only child. Brandy was as much a sister to her as she was companion, so taking Brandy with us was not an option. Ray's career at The Gap (yes, I still call it that, like an ancient) was skyrocketing. He was the "fix-it" guy always getting reassigned to the region that needed help. My career got put on to a back burner as I followed Ray around the country like a puppy. No complaining here. All of the city hopping and job jumping gave me the experience and confidence to become the founder of three businesses, but that is jumping ahead a few years.

Maryland, Virginia, Georgia and Illinois all flew by in rapid succession. We lived in Atlanta for exactly 29 days.

Once we settled into Los Angeles, we knew our relationship had traction and we both wanted to get a puppy. Fate intervened when a fellow employee announced her dog had given birth to puppies, purebred Dobermans—Ray's favorite breed.

We named her Kashi.

Kashi, six weeks old

The Gang of Eight

Kashi was so small and terrified when we brought her home. We cuddled her tightly to calm her fears. With a rare Los Angeles thunderstorm crashing loud enough to rattle windows all she wanted to do was to hide under the kitchen chair—a tall ladder-back chair with a tightly woven rush seat—handmade by my grandfather years earlier. Who were these strangers, she thought, and why is it so LOUD? Where were her mom and her brothers? Despite getting continually picked on by the gang of eight, she genuinely missed them. At just five weeks old, how could she possibly survive the night without the tangle of thirty-two tiny intertwined legs, the comforting warm breath of her siblings? With occasional outings for life's necessities, this is where she spent the first weekend in her new home. We tried coaxing her out, even trying to take her to bed with us that first night, but the chair was her safety zone.

She was adorable. All black with rust colored accents, her giant paws and floppy ears more than made up for her diminutive size. Her full name for the American Kennel Club was Takahashi—warrior in Japanese. I really don't know why we chose that name. She was definitely not very warrior-like in her early days, but it quickly got shortened to just Kashi—a smaller name for such a petite little girl. Even full grown she never weighed more than sixty-two pounds—very small for a Doberman. Despite her petite stature she was perfectly proportioned, often being mistaken for a show dog. When one Doberman breeder saw her, he immediately asked to use her to broaden his line of champions. He said everything about her was spot on and he was devastated when we informed him she had been spayed. "How could you do that to such a perfect animal?" he exclaimed. He was not satisfied with our answer involving overpopulation of dog shelters and left the conversation with great disappointment on his face.

As the days flew by in her new home, she got more comfortable and ventured out from the security of her chair discovering that, indeed, belly rubs and rawhide bones were a good trade-off. There was a big world out there waiting to be explored one mouthful at a time.

First to go was the carpet on the stairs followed by the curtains and the sofa. She ate the cushions, foam and all. We joked that her poop could bounce all the way to the doggie waste can. Her way to test the waters of something new was to put it into her mouth. This was an expensive habit that took us years to break and occasionally brought fear to the eyes of an unsuspecting guest when she gave them a "handshake" involving very large teeth grasping a dangling hand.

The pivotal point in our puppy parenting skills came the day she ate a light bulb out of the socket of a table lamp. Fifteen stitches later and a lot of cleanup, we beefed up our skills, cleared out all things tempting and left her during the day in our garage with a sofa, a radio tuned to a classical music station and an old rope buoy we found on the beach. Oh, how a crate would have changed our lives. But just as Ray and I survived childhood without benefit of seatbelts, Kashi survived her puppyhood.

While Kashi was still a youngster, we had her ears cropped. It was explained to us that a Doberman's ears are prone to infection and cropping them keeps them upright allowing the air to dry them naturally, avoiding yeast infections. Years later we found out that this is not entirely true and it is mostly done for appearance. What did we know? We were young. The AKC now accepts dogs into the show circuit with both styles of ears—natural and cropped. Kashi had difficulty healing from the surgery. Her incisions stayed raw for what seemed like forever. Many years later, a diagnosis of hypothyroidism explained her slow healing and small stature.

Kashi was allergic to the tape used to hold her ears upright in an "ear rack," which is a fancy name for a canine torture device looking similar to something that could receive signals from outer space. After several bouts of trial and error we finally found that cardboard tampon tubes wrapped with gauze worked well to keep her ears erect, yet dry and free of allergens. This was the dark ages when all tampons were made from cotton and came in a cardboard tube—boy does this make me feel old, like I am explaining the hand-cranked telephone. It was hard to explain to strangers when we walked her at the park why our dog had tampons stuck in her ears and even harder to answer the questions from four-year-olds. After "racking" our little girl for six months, her ears finally stayed upright, one at a time, and they were beautiful.

dog-ma

Kashi 1980 – 1996

six years old

Weapons of Mass Destruction

Kashi went with us everywhere. We had a Fiat X-19 with a removable hard top. How she loved riding with the top off; ears flapping, nose to the wind. We were incredibly naïve and lucky. We would park the car, top off, in a parking garage and leave her there for hours. No leash, nothing keeping her attached and nothing to keep anyone from stealing her. She would rather have waited alone in the car than be home alone. It would cause mild hysteria in the people who parked next to us when they would get out of their car, close their door and get a big smiling howdy-d-do from a Doberman. We certainly didn't need a car alarm.

Greeting us upon our return was always the trademark Kashi smile. She would see us across the parking lot, roll back her lips, show her teeth and smile. I don't know how she learned it, perhaps from observing us when we smiled at her.

Occasionally, strangers were terrified, but we knew better. She was a marshmallow trapped in a big scary body.

During the week, Kashi could go to work with Ray if he was working out of his office. She would stake out a spot on his sofa or under his conference table, greet visitors and watch meetings. His administrative assistant, Donna, was always gracious enough to take Kashi out for a potty break when necessary. One afternoon Ray was meeting with a group of managers and psychologists. It was a serious and detailed meeting that had everyone deeply engrossed. Donna was busy and had not noticed Kashi asking to go for a walk. Suddenly there was a gaseous release and the room was cleared in seconds; dignified professionals running from the room, hands covering noses, seeking breathable air. Her farts, which were surely strong enough to peel paint, could have been used as a new weapon of mass destruction.

Weekends were devoted to the beach. Dana Point was one of the few Los Angeles area beaches that allowed dogs to be off-leash. Kashi would race from the car to the water's edge, chase the seagulls and watch the surfers. In her head she could fly with the birds, generally resulting in a thudding belly flop in the sand. She would shake herself off and start it all over again. Her experience in chasing seagulls would define her life. She was tenacious to a fault. She viewed every day as a great adventure to be faced head-on with no regrets.

The beach was her paradise. Ray would coax her into the water slowly and let her bite at the waves as they rolled onto the beach. This became a favorite pastime. The surfers on the beach would laugh at her, which she apparently took as a personal challenge. It was not long before she taught herself to body surf. Every weekend for us was filled with beach trips and a sand-covered, exhausted dog. The surfers got to know her and looked forward to seeing her. Fun times. Quite interestingly, there is a cereal company— Kashi—that was started by a surfer from Dana Point around the same time. Coincidence in the name? We'll never know. I would like to believe her name was immortalized on a box of cereal.

Kashi's first year was filled with vet visits. Some visits were for the usual puppy stuff and some for emergencies. She was prone to getting ill; kidney infections, coughs, complications from her ear and spaying surgeries. The most frightening was Parvovirus. It was the early 1980's and Parvo was not well known. It is particularly deadly to young puppies causing both rapid and severe dehydration from diarrhea. At the time, it had an 80% fatality rate.

I had no idea she was severely ill, and thought she was just afflicted with a generalized upset stomach, not an unusual occurrence. She was the pickiest eater of dog food, but give her a pack of steel wool...now that was gourmet dining. I gave her a dose of Pepto Bismol and went to work. If she was not better by evening we would call the vet.

Midday, I was struck with a feeling of impending doom and thought it may be a good idea to go home and check on her. Kashi was lying on the floor panting, in serious distress, surrounded by vomit and bloody diarrhea, eyes rolled back in her head. I was terrified. I scooped her up and drove to the vet's office as fast as traffic would allow. Once there, he knew immediately what was wrong. He had a few clients with Parvo pups that week. He put her on IV fluids to treat her dehydration. There was no cure for Parvo in 1981. He told me to say my goodbyes. He would do what he could but said very few puppies survive.

I frantically called Ray who soon met me at the vet's office. We hugged her, told her we loved her and went home, hoping for a miracle. We found out many weeks later that the vet had decided he was not losing one more pup to Parvo that week. He took her home with him and sat up with her for two nights, kept her hydrated and tried to flush the virus out of her system. He knew she was a fighter. He watched her recover from ingesting a mouse that had eaten rat bait, just a month earlier. I know, I know...we deserved the bad parents of the year award. It took two weeks, but she made a full recovery from Parvo. Our little girl came home a bit skinnier but full of piss and vinegar.

Not All Doggies Have a Paddle

At about a year of age, she experienced our first home relocation from our rented townhouse to our first real home together. We were both divorced, and neither of us got to keep much from our marriages. We saved and saved and finally had our first down payment. It was a great moment in our relationship and we were very excited. As the movers packed our meager belongings on the moving truck, Kashi panicked. She watched as her dog sofa disappeared into the dark depths of the van. She paced, she panted, she whined. We did not understand why until we reached the new house and saw the dog sofa offloaded. Kashi's leapt from across the garage to her sofa. Ahhh. Now she was happy. The world was again in balance as she started chomping on the wooden sofa arm.

One of the many fun things about our new home was that it was in a new community where most homes were still vacant. Kashi could run off-leash without us worrying that she would disturb or frighten the neighbors. The community also had a pool that no one used but us. One night Ray took an evening swim while I walked Kashi. We stopped by to let him know we were on our way home. Kashi had never seen a swimming pool before. Her only experience with water was the ocean. She mistook Ray's swimming strokes as a struggle; her Doberman protection instincts ignited and she leapt into action. Kashi to the rescue...

As she raced across the concrete, past the pool edge and with feet still in a full gallop, she soared over the water until gravity prevailed. Belly first. As she broke the water's surface, the look of confused panic on her face is imbedded in my brain. What started as her rescue mission of Ray became Ray's rescue mission of Kashi. Our stomachs cramped from laughter. Her humiliation was evident as she snubbed us for the remainder of the evening. Years later when we bought a house with our own pool we never had to worry about her falling in. She kept her distance from the big wet monster that swallowed dogs.

We were so proud of our first home together and wanted to share it with our family that Christmas. We decided to fly Kristin, my parents, my sister and my grandparents to California to spend the holiday with us. Planning a day trip to Disneyland, we would leave very early in the morning and not return until very late at night. We did not want to leave Kashi home alone that long and made a day reservation for her in the Disneyland Kennel, which was a pretty darned fantastic place for a dog to spend the day. We could drop her off right at the entrance gate and she would be tended to and pampered all day long. She was to be bathed, massaged, and treated like royalty while we played in the park.

We rented a ten-passenger van for the trip and everyone piled in very excited to get to the theme park. My mom knew the stories of my dad's family selling their expanse of orange and walnut groves to Walt, the eccentric man who wanted to open an amusement park. She was also eager to see it, as well as our old family home that still sat across from the Disneyland entrance on Ball Road.

Kashi sensed everyone's excitement and as we pulled out of the garage, she hurled. Not just your everyday puppy vomit...no...this was projectile vomit shooting in a wide angled stream from the front of the van to the back windows. A scene from The Exorcist flashed through my head. I was horrified. My parents and grandparents, although dripping with vomit, felt worse for Kashi than they did for themselves. After showers, new attire and a trip to the full service carwash (where the attendants were generously tipped) we were off to Disneyland.

Never Assume People Can Read

Within a year, Ray accepted a promotion that took us to San Francisco. Once more, Kashi had to endure her sofa getting loaded onto a truck. This time, however, it was a garbage truck. We were not moving the chewed up remainder of what was once a beautiful sofa. We bought her a bed, putting it on the sofa for a week or so prior to the move to help ease her through the transition. As we hoped, when she saw her bed come off the moving truck and could curl up in it, the rest of the move was a non-event.

We had about a month before our new house would be livable. Floors needed refinished and painting needed done, so we chose to live in The Clift Hotel, an old-world elegant hotel in downtown San Francisco. This was long before the days of doggie hotels and doggie spas in hotels. Dogs were generally not allowed, but they made an exception for us (with some persuasion from Ray's company). The staff thought she was quite the novelty. The doorman took her for walks throughout the day. When we had room service dinner at night, the kitchen staff would bring her a bowl of food, a Milkbone and a note wishing her a "bone appetite." It seems so normal now, but in the eighties, this was amazing.

She was pampered to the extreme. Ray and I greatly appreciated it since we were both working long hours at our new jobs. Our days were filled with creating beautiful spaces. Our nights were filled with cleaning our own space, sparing the hotel maids. We asked for housekeeping to only tidy up and freshen the linens when we were in residence or took Kashi out for a stroll. We would leave the "do not disturb" sign on the doorknob as a reminder to the staff whenever Kashi was alone in the room.

Upon our return from work one evening we were greeted by a frenzied and apologetic night manager, wringing his hands in distress. He assured us that everything was now under control, but earlier in the day there had been "an incident." A new chambermaid had entered the room to clean, ignoring the "do not disturb" sign on the door. Kashi was a very quiet dog. For the first year of her life we actually thought she couldn't bark. The poor defenseless chambermaid decided to start her cleaning routine in the bathroom and had not noticed Kashi sleeping in her bed under the desk. As she scrubbed the fixtures, Kashi got up to get a drink. Why no one responded to the maid's blood-curdling scream is beyond me, but no one came to her rescue. She locked herself in the bathroom only to be found hours later when her supervisor realized she was missing. Note to self: never assume people read signs.

Kashi loved our new San Francisco house. It was the first time she had a doggie door. She could go in and out at will, anytime she wanted a little fresh air or when nature called. The back yard was fenced and gated and we knew she would be very safe. We left the doggie door open for her day or night and it really helped us to feel less guilty about leaving her alone on long work days. In the rear of the yard there was a tall cement retaining wall. Like most of San Francisco, our house was built on a hill. The neighborhood raccoons used the wall as their own personal highway. It was high enough that even at a good jump Kashi could not reach the top. The raccoons and Kashi made peace with each other.

It was not the same story for an ironically named big black cat who lived across the street. Brownie thought it was fun to sit on top of the wall and taunt Kashi. He would flick his tail, just out of Kashi's reach, day after day, week after week. One night the garden gate was accidentally left open. When we realized Kashi was missing we scouted the neighborhood, finding her safely curled up on our front porch sporting a look that can only be described as a smirk. To our horror, a few days later we noticed Brownie had just a bandage-wrapped stub where his tail had been. That tail never flicked at Kashi again. Poor Brownie. With a hermit mom who planted plastic flowers in her garden, there was not much hope for a prosthetic tail. A generous donation to the Humane Society left us feeling somewhat less guilty about our suspicion of the source of the missing tail. Many years later, while driving down our former street, there he was. Brownie was still wandering the 'hood and proudly strutting with his Manx-like silhouette.

All Aboard!

Closing the garden gate proved to be a continual challenge for the gardener and Kashi seemed to have radar that knew the minute it was not shut. I spent many days searching the neighborhood for her. While preparing to leave for work one morning I discovered she was gone again. AARGH!

Panic swept over me as I drove further and further through the neighborhood to no avail. I spotted a nice elderly couple out for a walk. They had noticed a big black dog heading toward Ocean Avenue. I raced down the hill. She had never strayed that far before. Ocean Avenue was a very busy street with not only cars but also MUNI and BART tracks. What if she crossed traffic and got hit by a car or a train? Would someone stop and help her? How would I find her? What if she was headed off to the beach? Ocean Beach was within walk-able distance and the waves were not as gentle as the waves at Dana Point. The undertow here was like a suction cup, instantly stealing anything loose from the shoreline and carrying it out to sea.

Fortunately she was a very friendly dog and stopped to say hello to everyone she passed. I found a few more folks who had passed her and kept on her trail. I parked and went on foot arriving at the MUNI station just as the doors on the train were getting ready to close. Guess who was sitting in a seat like it was totally normal for a dog to get a seat on the train? The other passengers were laughing uncontrollably, the conductor was not all together pleased, but I did get him to crack a smile when I told him she mistakenly thought she was late for work when she actually had the day off. I gathered her up in my arms, kissed her and took her home. That night the gate got a combination padlock.

Sadly, the lock on the garden gate was not the end of our dog door woes. The worst was a wake-up call that occurred around 3:00 AM, when we were abruptly wakened by Kashi's panicked jump into the middle of our bed accompanied by a dreadful wail that sounded more like a dying whale than a dog. "What is that smell?" we both said in unison. Then it hit us...SKUNK!!

She had taken a direct hit, face first. She must have strolled out to take an early morning walk and found a cute little furry thing roaming the yard. HER yard. What could she do but give it a proper doggie greeting—a butt sniff. The acrid spray was in her eyes, up her nose, it had eaten the paint off of her collar and tags and now the smell was on the floor, the bedding and us. Ray grabbed her and held her in the bathtub. We could barely breathe. The smell was burning our eyes. I frantically searched the kitchen for anything with tomatoes in it. Not cooking much in those days, the cupboards were pretty bare. Then I remembered...PASTA SAUCE! Ragu saved us that night. We packed it on her, on us, scrubbed the floor with it. It was months before we got out that smell. Sheets and blankets—trash. Pillows—trash. Mattress—trash. Towels and shower curtain—trash. Our cleaning woman performed magic, but this was way beyond her pay grade. She told us she would come back when the smell was gone. We never saw her again.

The Night Stalker

From April 1984 to August 1985, The Night Stalker terrorized California from San Diego to San Francisco. He would break into homes in the middle of the night, beat the occupants, rape the women and kill them either by beating or shooting them. Richard Ramirez now awaits execution in San Quentin State Penitentiary being found guilty on thirteen counts of murder, five attempted murders, eleven sexual assaults and fourteen burglaries.

On the night of August 17, 1985, I was sound asleep, tucked safely in our bed with Kashi at my feet. Ray was away on a business trip. Around midnight I awoke to Kashi quietly but urgently licking my face as if to say "mom, get up." Once I was awake she bolted for her dog door and hit it with a thud at a high rate of speed, teeth gnashing. I had never heard her make a sound like that before, a combination gurgle, bark and snarl. It was a ferocious sound and it terrified me. I ran to the window and there she was, viciously struggling below a man who was trying to scale our back wall, with his pant leg in her mouth. She would not let go until she received a few hard kicks in the face. He got away.

I called the police and also our neighbor, Frank, who was a retired FBI agent. Frank and his wife arrived first, still in their pajamas. He searched the yard and surrounding area and found only footprints and some shreds of fabric, probably from the intruder's trousers. Kashi would not come inside. She was going to guard that wall and protect her home. Lights popped on in most of the homes on our street. Her barking made quite a commotion. The police felt the lack of an alarm made our house a target for the would-be burglar and were confident that with the sudden appearance of a Doberman, the intruder would most likely never come back. It took hours for her to calm down. I felt safe with her watching over me and we finally got some sleep.

In the evening, when I returned from work, I turned on the news and was enveloped in shock. A man and his wife, Barbara and Peter Pan living in Park Merced, a neighborhood next to ours, were attacked during the night. Peter had been killed; Barbara had been raped, beaten and badly injured. The suspect was Richard Ramirez, The Night Stalker. I called Frank and he confirmed that Kashi probably saved my life.

Worst Dog Parents on the Planet

With Ray's new position as a Vice President of The Gap, he received many party invitations. One invitation was for San Francisco's first Black Tie & Sneakers Garbage Ball. It was a benefit for AIDS Research held at the Marin County Landfill. In Marin, California, even the garbage is posh. As usual, we took Kashi with us. She would be quite content waiting for us in the car. Maybe we would stop on the way home and get her favorite treat: an ice cream cone!

We did not know that fireworks would be a part of the evening entertainment. Kashi was in the car with the sunroof open while fireworks exploded overhead. We raced to the car, but not in time. Among the burned remnants of fireworks paper on the floor was Kashi, terrified. The fireworks had mistakenly been shot toward the parking lot and went off too low. The fear of booms would haunt her for the rest of her life. We never forgave ourselves for the shock she endured. Years later we would have to take turns sitting in the closet with her when thunder claps got too loud.

The Big Kahuna

Every Sunday we went to Louie's on Ocean Beach for brunch. We loved their omelets and at the time it was an old locals hangout, not a tourist restaurant. Back in the days before Starbuckanization, we thought they had awesome coffee. Sitting on the bluff directly above the Sutro Bath ruins we always had a great view and a relaxing morning. It became a routine for us.

Kashi could smell the beach as we drove toward Louie's and would start to vocalize her wish to go surfing. It would start out as a small whine and grow to the intensity of an air raid siren. If she didn't get her way and get taken to the beach we paid the price in deafness. She was not happy until brunch was finished and she was running on the sand.

The water in San Francisco was much colder than in Southern California but that didn't stop Kashi. She loved to body surf. The major difference on Ocean Beach was that Kashi could not run free.

There were leash laws in San Francisco and the undertow on the beach was often very violent. One sunny afternoon, the undertow grabbed her as she chased a wave.

Ray felt the tug on her long line and it was fierce. He was afraid that if he pulled her in too quickly he would pull off her collar and lose her forever. Then she disappeared under a wave. Ray did not see her surface but he still felt tension on the leash and it was moving forward. He walked down the beach holding the leash tightly. There was Kashi swimming parallel to the beach, escaping the undertow.

We never taught her that and have no idea how she knew to do it; perhaps it was luck or instinct and perhaps it was something else. Ray helped her as she swam onto the beach, flopping onto the sand with exhaustion. They both sat in the sand for a long time, Kashi catching her breath so she could go back after another wave, Ray thanking the Big Kahuna, guardian angel of all surfers.

The Invisible Man

The following summer found Ray a bit bored with his job at The Gap. He had successfully developed and opened the first round of Gap Kids stores and was ready to take on a new venture when he was offered a position with a new company in Los Angeles. It was my favorite city and I was thrilled. San Francisco had been too cold and gray for me. Being a fellow sun worshiper, Kashi shared my enthusiasm. Our new Bell Canyon home was magnificent and Kashi got acclimated instantly. We had a pool with a Jacuzzi connected by a 20-foot waterfall and stream. Kashi lay in the stream, in the sun, catching some rays and staying cool. Her favorite pastime was chasing the tail of the pool sweeper as it lurched out of the water. She could amuse herself for hours and it was great exercise. Every once in a while she would catch it, almost get pulled into the pool and the chase was on again. I always wondered if she thought that was the monster from the deep that almost got her years earlier.

Even in the 1980's traffic in Los Angeles was brutal. Our daily commute to work took us an hour, sometimes an hour and a half each way. Fortunately our jobs were situated close and we could drive together, Ray to Santa Monica and I to Century City. Many nights we stopped at a favorite restaurant for dinner not arriving home until well past 10:00 PM. Kashi was home alone a lot. We talked about it for weeks and finally decided to visit the Los Angeles Doberman Rescue to see if we could find a suitable buddy for her. Big problem. Kashi had been with us since she was five weeks old and went everywhere with us. She thought she was a person, not a dog. We arrived on a Saturday and explained our purpose to the wonderful woman manning the shelter that morning. She understood and said we were welcome to walk Kashi through the kennels to see if she found a dog to her liking.

The vast quantity of unwanted Dobermans made us sad. Some were young, some were old. They all needed a forever home, but Kashi was not warming up to any of them. We walked her past cage after cage for an hour with no luck. She snubbed every dog and kept giving us a defiant look. Maybe we had interpreted her loneliness wrong and she didn't want a buddy. We stopped at the office to say goodbye and to thank them for being so understanding.

As we walked through the office door her stubby tail started to wag uncontrollably, like a metronome on steroids. On the floor sat The Invisible Man; a six month old male Dobie covered in bandages. The shelter woman explained he was not up for adoption. He had been abandoned there just a few days earlier, chained to their front fence in the early morning hours. He had just been neutered, had both his dew claws removed, tail docked and ears cropped. He was a bloody mess, quite literally. As we talked, we could not believe what we were seeing. Kashi was on the floor licking him, nudging him and apparently trying to comfort him. It was amazing and brings tears to my eyes, even today. Kashi had found her soul mate.

We named him Turbo.

Turbo 1986 – 1995

two years old

Spock Ears

What a big bundle of energy. Even with his bandages he was moving non-stop. Turbo was a perfect name. We immediately removed the bandages from his ears. We did not need or even want his ears to stand up straight. Ear cropping is cruel. However, since they were already cropped, the least we could do was let them heal naturally in the air. Who cared if his ears flopped over? We were not going to let this puppy go through the torture Kashi had endured. Floppy ears, so be it. Well, the joke was on us. Even though the surgery on his ears was only a week old, those ears stood straight up like perfect little soldiers, angled and pointy making him look like Mr. Spock.

Turbo's feet were huge and he had typical puppy clumsiness. Some days he would run after Kashi and trip, rolling into a ball of tumbling feet. We lived on an acre of land, completely enclosed with white equestrian fence. It was a perfect yard for the two of them to explore together. We had large outcroppings of rocks that they liked to race to the top of to survey the world in the valley below. There were partridges to chase and coyotes to avoid. Every so often, a horse and rider would travel down the bridal trail that ran between all properties in the Canyon. They loved the horses, never barking, but running alongside them as though they were challenging them to a race.

As Turbo grew, he started to get restless being confined to the yard and began digging holes, allowing him to escape under the fence. Kashi was too well behaved to participate in those shenanigans. Turbo never went far, usually sitting just on the other side of the fence. He had issues with confinement. Not wanting to take any chances, we called the fence company and had them attach a wire fence to the inside of the horse fence and bury it two feet underground. That ought to keep him in, we thought.

HA! Not our Turbo. He was an explorer-man, an adventurer, a wild thing. He was unrelenting in his desire to escape. In less than a week he learned how to open the gate with his mouth. We had no idea the two of them were wandering the neighborhood during the day. Fortunately Bell Canyon was a box canyon with no escape and the main road was gated, with guards. As the dogs explored, they discovered a home where a lovely man and his wife lived about a half of a mile up the hill from our home. Kashi and Turbo, or the Germans, as we liked to refer to them since they were a breed from Germany, would go to their house every afternoon, get some water and treats, visit, take a nap and then the couple, having read the address on their ID tags, would walk them home and put them back in the yard. This went on for months, unknown to us until the afternoon we came home early and saw a couple walking down our road with the Germans in tow. We apologized profusely that the dogs had caused them trouble. They laughed and relayed the story of how long it had been going on. They loved to get their afternoon visit and enjoyed the walk down to our home. It continued until the day we moved.

Other neighbors also thought the Germans were a kick. In our neighborhood novelty was celebrated. Across the street was Jamie Farr, Klinger from M*A*S*H, and his family; also, at the end of our road lived former Wonder Woman Lynda Carter. Ray and Turbo loved jogging at the same time as Lynda...MEN! Just up the road from us was a wonderfully authentic adobe-style ranch house with stables and a corral built from the earnings of the ZZ Top "Fandango!"

record album. The home had been named Fandango Ranch. Bill, its owner, had quite the sense of humor. He had a stuffed cow in his living room on wheels so he could lasso it. The toilet room in his master bathroom had a set of outhouse doors. They had several horses and a goat. Every afternoon the goat would take a horse out for a walk down the street and occasionally Turbo would join them. We had colorful neighbors. It was never a surprise to get a phone call saying the Dobermans had crashed another party and were raiding the hotdogs and drinking the beer. Everyone knew them and enjoyed their company.

The Head
Bangers Ball

We were in the process of selling our Bell Canyon home so that Ray could accept a position running a company in Seattle. The real estate agent called saying we had a celebrity interested in looking at our home and he wanted anonymity. That's kind of hard to do in a gated community in Los Angeles, but we worked with it in hopes that they would love our home as we had and buy it. Ray and I left for an hour to let Mr. Celebrity look at our home privately.

The viewing went well and the real estate agent called to tell us to come home. When we arrived we were introduced to Vince Neil, from Motley Crue and his girlfriend Celeste. What a nice guy—nothing like his reputation. They loved the house but the rest of his "band mates" would need to approve. He asked permission for them all to come over to look around. Permission? Seriously? Within the hour, three more heavily tattooed and pierced people arrived along with their drop-dead beautiful girlfriends. Vince also brought his dad, which I thought was sweet.

It was hilarious to watch these "bad boys" rolling around on the living room floor with the Germans. They seemed more interested in the dogs than the house. The dogs really liked these guys and they were both excellent judges of character. Just like our dogs, the guys looked mean and scary but were really softies under their gruff exteriors. Our neighbors got a lopsided trade. The Wandering Germans were gone and the Head Bangers arrived. Years later we ran into Jamie Farr in an elevator in NYC where he let us know, quite comically, how much the Germans were missed... Apparently the 'hood had gotten a bit noisy.

Foofing

Out of Turbo's "life before us" came a fear of vehicles. Just sitting in the car in the garage would cause him to hyperventilate and make a sound that would become known as "foofing." He inhaled great quantities of air, and then quickly and repeatedly blew it out causing his cheeks to fill up like a blow-fish.

He was terrified when we needed to take him to the vet. It was a trip that took two of us: both to get him in the car, one to drive and one to sit and hold his head. It was a fear we would help him to manage but he would never fully conquer.

In later years while we were on a road trip across country, we started to suspect that he could have belonged to a truck driver who treated him poorly and then abandoned him. He panicked in a Wisconsin truck stop while we were getting gas, parked next to the truck diesel fuel pumps. He heard a truck engine start up and took off at a full gallop. I will never forget the look of terror in his eyes as he darted in between cars and trucks, heading for the highway.

Happy endings...a few friendly truckers helped us capture him and get him back in the car. We were much more conscientious about closing the car door when we filled up after that.

Turbo's first major hurdle with foofing came when we moved from Bell Canyon to Seattle. It was a three-day car trip. We worked with him for weeks prior to the move. Treats were good motivation to jump into the car but nothing worked to keep him calm. He was simply petrified. On moving day we kept a close eye on him as the truck was packed with all of our belongings. We kept the dog beds in the car so he had a familiar scent and didn't go through the same panic as Kashi had the first time she saw her sofa go onto the moving truck. By now Kashi was a seasoned mover. As long as she had her dog bed and a favorite toy she was happy. The truck was packed and it was time for us to go. With great trepidation we loaded the Germans into the car and we were off to our new Seattle home.

The first day of our trip required one of us to sit in the back seat with Turbo and hold his head while he foofed and whined. Kashi got the front seat and judging from the smirk on her face was decidedly happy about the seating arrangements. By Day Two he jumped in the car voluntarily and we took that as a good sign. Enjoying a fast food breakfast, he probably thought "okay, this isn't so bad?" He foofed occasionally throughout the day, mostly when we stopped for gas, but he made it. Day Three...he got in the car without a struggle, sat on his bed and fell fast asleep. Victory!! Foofing was rarely heard again.

barbara boswell brunner

Yummy. Old Shoes!

Our Seattle home was not really in Seattle, we just generically referred to it that way. We were actually in Bellevue across Lake Washington from Seattle; a small town made famous by a college dropout who started up a little computer software company. The Bellevue house sat on a hill at the end of a street of ten homes in a neighborhood called Bridal Trails. At the entrance to the street were two houses with stables, corrals and of course beautiful horses. This was a great setting for the dogs and not too unfamiliar. They had lots of space to run throughout the house, up and down three levels. They had their own doggie room complete with a huge picture window, sofa and dog door.

Their dog run was enclosed under the second floor deck and would keep them dry in the rain but still let them feel like they could get outdoors. We had the concrete pad poured and fence installed before we arrived so the dogs could start using it immediately. We didn't want to take any chances with them getting loose in an unfamiliar city.

Turbo was still having issues with confinement. He took every opportunity to escape. He never went far—usually just around our property. He would come to the deck door when he was ready to come back in and we got in the habit of letting him out every evening for a run. He needed to stretch his legs and satisfy his wandering spirit. He began traveling down the street and visiting the horses.

There were both horses AND kids and we did not know how Turbo would be around children. He was never exposed to them but we found out one afternoon when we looked out and saw the neighborhood kids riding him like a horse. He seemed to be having a blast but this had to stop. He could run out into the street and get hit by a car or scare someone who did not know that inside his one hundred pound body was a snuggly little teddy bear. We stopped letting him wander unaccompanied. He was so miserable that Ray took up jogging again so the two of them could wear off some of that energy. It worked for a while.

One afternoon we came home to discover BOTH dogs were missing. Turbo had GNAWED through the chain link and pulled back a section to make a getaway hole like a skilled Alcatraz escapee. This time Kashi was with him. We searched the street and the surrounding neighborhoods. They had not taken off together since their days in Bell Canyon. That was a safe neighborhood. This one was just blocks from the freeway's edge and a mile from a major interchange. So many horrible thoughts went through our minds.

Turbo had admirable street smarts, but Kashi...not so much. She would wander in a straight line until she got tired, which in her youth could be a very long time. We searched and searched. They were nowhere. We jumped in the car and started searching the outer roads of Bridal Trails, up the hills, down long driveways. We were ready to give up and call the police when suddenly they appeared, lying under a tree at the freeways edge, over a mile from home. Kashi was napping and Turbo chomping on an old shoe he had found. To this day I do not think this was a voluntary march for Turbo. I suspect Kashi started walking and he followed to protect her. When they got to the freeway I imagine him saying "ENOUGH—now sit down, shut up and wait for mom and dad." He was such a good boy. Invisible Fence came to our rescue and the dogs never left the yard again.

barbara boswell brunner

Pee-apalooza

The Germans were joined at the hip. They looked out after each other, protected each other and got each other into lots of trouble. Kashi taught Turbo the art of eating shoes. Ray's shoes were a special delicacy, with the left shoe being much tastier than the right. Turbo discovered eating eyeglasses and remote controls all on his own. The one behavior Kashi could not tolerate was Turbo's poor bathroom habits. We had great difficulty getting him to stop peeing in the living room. We even hired a trainer. Her genius solution was to fill an empty soda can with a few pennies and throw it at him when he stepped across the threshold. "That'll keep him out" she declared.

Yea, not so much. She threw the can, he was terrified at the noise and started running around peeing on the wall as he ran. As our housekeeper, Taiko, ran after him yelling in Japanese, I tried to grab him. It was a circus. Kashi stood in the doorway, hung her head in disgust, turned and left the room. Eventually we found a piece of aluminum foil placed strategically in the doorway was deterrent enough. My father found this extraordinarily funny when he would visit. He couldn't imagine such a big dog would be afraid of a little piece of foil.

Turbo also had a way of expressing his true feelings with pee. We had a frequent houseguest that he was not fond of, Stephanie. She worked with Ray but lived in Southern California. When she traveled to Seattle she always stayed with us to save the company a hotel bill. We enjoyed her company but apparently Turbo did not. One evening she was sitting in the library reading while Ray and I had a meeting in the kitchen with some folks who were working on a project for us. We heard a muffled scream coming from the library followed by Stephanie scurrying into the kitchen to find a rag.

"What's wrong?" we asked. "That...that dog...that DOG" pointing at Turbo, teeth clenched, with a hint of spittle on her lips, trying to hold back her obvious anger. "He came into the library and I thought he wanted his ears scratched. As I was patting him he peed on my leg." We were mortified, but also chuckled silently as we cleaned up the mess. Stephanie never stayed with us again. I said he was a good judge of character!

And The Winner Is...

Ray received a job offer he couldn't refuse, Chief Executive Officer of a design and retail firm in New York City. It was his dream job. Although I had only recently founded my own business, after great discussion we decided he could not pass up the opportunity. While our house was on the market in Bellevue, Ray rented an apartment on East 63rd, in the heart of Manhattan. I traveled back and forth house hunting and trying to hire someone to run my business while we were in New York. With our track record for moving I figured I would need someone for a year or two and we'd be back in Seattle. Fortunately Kristin, my step daughter, was living with us in Bellevue and could babysit the dogs and help keep an eye on my business, even working there a few nights a week.

Our house hunting focused on Connecticut. Ray grew up in the area and knew it well. We would have enough space for the dogs to run and his commute into New York City would not be untenable; forty-five minutes on Metro North. We found a wonderful home—very Norman Rockwell-ish—in downtown Ridgefield, Connecticut. We could walk to the restaurants and coffee shops. It was ideal. Before we made the move, we had Invisible Fence come and install a new underground fence for us to avoid the problems we had in Bellevue. We kept our fingers crossed that it would keep the dogs contained and discourage them from chasing the deer.

It worked beautifully. Our only wish was that we could have put Invisible Fence collars on the deer to keep them OUT. The dogs and the deer made peace with each other, although I cannot say the same for our rhododendron bushes.

We didn't have the luxury of being able to take a week to drive the dogs to their new home. Ray already had his feet on the ground in the new job. I did not want to risk driving with both dogs alone, cross country in the winter, so we decided to fly them to New York.

What troopers! Kashi was already a seasoned flyer having traveled with us to the East Coast several years before. Turbo, we weren't as confident with. If his foofing returned, it could cause a heart attack.   At the suggestion of our veterinarian, we fed him a small meal of cheese laced with sedatives and he was loaded onto the plane for a non-stop flight to JFK Airport. The airline promised to keep their crates together so they could see each other and evidently they did because when we claimed the Germans in oversized baggage Turbo was perfectly fine, a little sleepy, very happy to get out of the crate, but fine.

The closing on our Connecticut home would not be for a few days so we took a room at the Hilton Hotel in Manhattan. We were surprised to find out that dogs were quite welcome. There were even doggie treats waiting for them in the room.   How sweet!   We got the dogs settled and after a short rest it was time to take them for a walk around New York City.

It was February, there was snow on the ground and it was beautiful. We got into the elevator and the folks who were already in the car wished us luck. How nice, we thought. We exited into the lobby and the doorman gave us directions on where to walk the dogs and also wished us luck. Did they know something we didn't? It seemed odd but nice nonetheless. The same thing happened to us every time we went in and out of the hotel with the dogs.

Only later did we realize it was the week of the Westminster Dog Show. They thought the Germans were in the Dog Show! I still giggle when I think about it. Turbo? As a show dog? Only if it were a Herman Munster look-a-like show or perhaps Comic-Con. He was the sweetest dog, but only his mother would call him handsome.

Connecticut was a great home for the dogs. They loved their huge yard, loved taking walks downtown and we found out they both loved the snow. They would romp outside for hours and then come in and warm themselves by the fire. I worked from morning to night with a phone attached to my ear keeping track of my business. I set up an office on our third floor and kept the dogs running all day going up and down three flights of stairs. They were livin' large. With mom home all day long, a yard with lots of stuff to chase, a warm fire at night, we had happy kids.

We spent so much time in our yard tending to new landscaping. Kashi and Turbo were always by our side. They loved to chase each other around the house and jump into piles of leaves or grass clippings that had been freshly raked. There were many holes to explore and deer poop to roll in.

Connecticut is where the dogs first met Joe and Sally. Joe had worked with Ray years before and Ray recruited him to work with him again, at his new job in New York. I knew Joe slightly but had never met his wife. We invited them to join us for dinner at one of the local restaurants and decided to meet at our home first for cocktails. I new she was nervous meeting me for the first time, as I was her.

Sally looked like Goldie Hawn when she arrived at the door, wearing a gorgeous white ensemble, perfectly coifed and manicured. As she and Joe walked through the doorway, Kashi and Turbo came bounding from the back yard, covered in mud from a new hole they were exploring and without warning both jumped up on Sally to greet her. I shrieked and was mortified that this stunning woman and her outfit were now covered in mud. What an introduction. Instead of gasping or yelling "my outfit" Sally giggled, sat down on the floor and buried herself in puppy kisses. I knew at that moment, we would be friends for life.

Ray loved working for Terrance, the founder of Conran's Habitat, but venture vultures grabbed it in a hostile takeover, forcing Terrance out. Ray had no desire to stay without Terrance at the helm. Seattle beckoned, this time a lake house in

Redmond. It was wintertime. We loved to ski so we decided to take a long road trip and ski our way across America. We threw the dogs in our Porsche, strapped the skis to the roof and set out on the adventure of a lifetime. We stopped at all of the national monuments, took photos of the dogs in front of Mt. Rushmore and in the Badlands. We skied to our hearts content and the dogs got to play in the snow all the way across the country. Sally and Joe followed just a few months later moving into a home just a mile or so from us.

The Germans posing at Mt. Rushmore

Broken Hearts

We noticed on that trip that Turbo had developed a cough. It didn't seem too bad, but a couple of times a day he would hack, a very wet hack. Sometimes it seemed like he was having trouble catching his breath, especially when Ray took him running. We took him to the vet the dogs had gone to from the time we originally moved to Seattle. Dr. Randy was concerned. He remembered how robust Turbo had been before our Connecticut move and wasn't seeing that anymore. He wanted Turbo to see a cardiologist. He was only seven years old. Turbo was diagnosed with cardiomyopathy, a deterioration of the function of the myocardium—heart muscle disease. His heart could no longer pump properly and his lungs were filling with fluid. His heart was broken, and so were ours. The cardiologist told us Turbo had perhaps two or three weeks to live. He prescribed medicine to help his heart function a bit better and to eliminate excess fluids. He was taking seventeen very expensive pills every day to keep him alive. They were human medicines and of course not covered by insurance, but we wanted to give him the most comfortable last weeks we could. It would only be a couple of weeks...or so we thought.

Kashi and Turbo had always played hard. They ran together, chased stuff together and wrestled. Chest-butting was a favorite pastime. They were always on the go and now Turbo didn't have any energy. Just going outside to the bathroom exhausted him. Kashi still wanted to play non-stop and made up different games for them. She would run around him, letting him lie still and she would pounce on him or they would mouth wrestle, making the most horribly ferocious noises. If you didn't know they were just playing it could be intimidating. She also taught him how to play tug of war in a way that he didn't have to move. She was a good nurse and his best friend. They adapted. That's what friends do.

Two weeks became two months. Two months turned into two years. We were astounded. Turbo had such a will to survive. We had some close calls. Business trips required us to board the dogs. Academy of Canine Behavior in Woodinville, Washington, was a wonderful kennel and knew Turbo's medical history well. One day while boarding, Turbo went into cardiac arrest. The kennel man threw him into his truck and raced at top speed to our vet's office, which was just a couple of miles away. He said he never looked at his speedometer and was actually hoping for a cop. His wish came true, flashing lights appeared behind him and he was pulled over for speeding. After quickly explaining the problem, he got a safe escort, lights and siren all the way. He recognized the problem, didn't panic (until later recounting the story) and got Turbo the help he needed. The kennel man never got a ticket for speeding. He saved Turbo's life.

Joe and Sally were at our home or we at theirs on a weekly basis. We shared a love of good food, wine, and animals. They owned a wine store while living in San Francisco and taught us so much about wine appreciation and food pairings. They are directly responsible for our uncontrollable desire to keep a well-stocked wine cellar. In case of world collapse, there will be no shortage of alcohol at our homes. They had their own brood of pets including cats, dogs, and Bugsy, a rabbit who became hypnotized when you rubbed his belly. Sally even adopted a deer when we lived in Connecticut.

As Turbo became more ill, we relied on them to housesit for us when business called us out of town. We did not want to take chances boarding Turbo. Because of his illness, he had stopped getting his vaccinations and being around other dogs could expose him to infections he could not fight. Sally would come in the morning, feed them and visit with them all day. She would go home after they were fed their dinner and put to bed for the night.

On a Saturday morning, both Sally and Joe came for early morning dog duty. The dogs were in the yard to greet them as they came through the gate. That was unusual, they both thought. It was pretty cold outside. They exited the car and were greeted by two very wet dogs. Now things seemed exceptionally odd. It was not raining. As they proceeded to open the front door, the dogs kept their distance and Joe thought oh no... what have they done? Water was EVERYWHERE! The entire first floor was flooded with several inches of water. Neither Kashi nor Turbo would come inside. They stood on the porch with each on opposite sides of the doorframe; peeking around the corner as if to say, "Don't know how THAT happened...we didn't do it. Nope, nope, not us."

Poor Joe! He discovered that the hot water heater had blown a valve during the night and water had been flowing into the house non-stop for hours. Fortunately the dogs slept upstairs and probably only discovered the flood in the morning. As he tried to figure out how to get the mess cleaned up, Kashi started to play in the water. Romping around, splashing water onto everything that was not already wet. Ah ha. That's how they got so wet. They thought they had their own personal splash pool in the living room. They could turn the worst situations into a game and have fun. If we humans had that same ability to always find the silver lining, the world would be a better place.

While dog sitting, Sally also had the responsibility of getting seventeen pills a day down Turbo's throat. Because of his tendency to gain weight easily and the need to keep his weight low for his heart condition, he could not be given pills in a treat like cheese. They had to be dropped down his throat; intimidating for someone whose biggest dog is smaller than most handbags. Sally came for a couple of days prior to our trip to practice and was very anxious. She wasn't sure she could do it, but she was a champ, braving the big Doberman teeth, holding his jaw open and dropping pills one at a time down his throat. Turbo seemed to sense her fear and behaved like a gentleman, allowing Sally to give him his pills with ease. By the time the week was over, Turbo held his mouth open so Sally didn't need to hold his head. He was such a good boy.

Taking Turbo to the cardiologist every week was my task but on a week when I was not available, Ray had dog duty. Coincidently, the regular cardiologist Turbo had been seeing was on vacation and there was another vet taking his place that week. Since Ray had not taken him before and this vet was new to the case, the vet wanted to confirm with Ray what medicines Turbo was taking. He would say "...so he is taking one of such and such a medicine," and "he takes two of such and such a medicine."

Each time Ray corrected him and said, no he takes four of those and six of these, etc. Well, it turns out that Turbo was taking WAY more medicine than what was originally prescribed. The cardiologist had sloppy handwriting on the original prescription or the pharmacist read the prescription wrong but either way their mistake had given us extra time with Turbo that we did not expect to have. We were told that because of the mistake, changes were being suggested for veterinarian schools on how much medication a dog with heart disease can tolerate. Hopefully someone else also benefited by getting more time with his or her beloved pet because of a simple pharmaceutical error.

When Ray was diagnosed with hypertrophic cardiomyopathy many years later, we were armed with plenty of knowledge about the condition through our experience with Turbo. I still find it crazy that those two guys, with the same genetic heart condition, jogged together for so many years and neither of them dropped over from a heart attack. It's just crazy...and lucky...

Several months later Turbo was having more and more difficulty breathing. We took him to Dr. Randy for shots to help clear his lungs. He would be fine for a few weeks and then he would need another. Soon the shots were needed every few days. Dr. Randy told us it was finally time to say goodbye. Turbo's system could not handle any more diuretics. We weren't prepared. Turbo was not ready to go. He pleaded to us with his eyes not to leave him. He looked terrified, as though he knew what was coming next. Almost two years to the day that he was diagnosed with a heart problem, Turbo was gone.

We asked to be with him when he was euthanized, and Dr. Randy said no. With all of the fluid buildup in his lungs it would be messy and he did not want us to remember him that way. We will regret that decision forever. The image burned into our brains is of Turbo's pleading eyes, as he was led to the back room. We sat in the car in the parking lot and sobbed. We were lucky to have had him in our lives and we would miss him forever.

Kashi mourned, extraordinarily so. She missed Turbo. We knew it would be hard for her to find another buddy. She didn't like other dogs. Maybe it was best to stay with one dog, we thought. She continued to mope; not eating, not playing. She walked with her head hung low and her shoulders hunched. She lost weight and did not have any extra pounds to lose. After a few weeks it became clear we had to do something or we would lose her to heartbreak.

You Have To See Him NOW!

Bellevue Square, the Seattle area's largest shopping mall had a pet shop. Not a puppy mill shop. They used local breeders and shelter dogs and it was all very legitimate, clean and well run. While I worked with the staff of my shop, Ray would visit the puppies. There was one he had fallen in love with but someone else had already adopted it. Suddenly the puppy was back—the buyer had returned him. It baffles me how people can do that, return a pet like it was an expired carton of milk, but Ray was thrilled. He raced back to my shop to tell me.

"Why was it returned?" I inquired. "I don't know but you've got to come and see him, NOW." Not really being on board with another dog, I slowly sauntered upstairs to the pet shop. "Hurry," Ray said. "Someone else might adopt him. They are holding him in the playroom."

Now, being the eternal pessimist that I am, I knew there had to be something wrong with this dog. Anyway, Ray never said what KIND of puppy it was. Hmmm. On the floor of the playroom sat the cutest bundle of black and tan fur that I had ever seen, a big puppy belly and huge rust colored eyebrows.

"Ray...it's a Rottweiler! I will not have a baby-killing Rottweiler in my house and that's final."

"Just sit down on the floor with him for a minute," Ray pleaded. I sat on the floor and that little munchkin wobbled up onto my lap and I fell head over heels in love. We named him Lexington.

It was obvious the pet shop manager loved this little adorable ball of fur. Lexington had been at the shop for almost four months. The manager would let him run around the shop when it was closed and Lexi developed a great affection for a lop-eared rabbit. He carried the bunny around in his mouth like a stuffed animal, he would nuzzle it and they would play. He was a gentle dog, very sweet and thoughtful.

The manager said Lexington had been returned because it was discovered he had mild hip dysplasia and the young woman who bought him wanted a running companion. Ok, we thought. We can deal with mild dysplasia and were hoping just a few simple pain relievers would be all it would take to keep him comfortable. Before we made a final decision, though, Kashi would have to give her approval. Conveniently, Ray had her in the car in the parking lot. Hmmm...I started to suspect maybe this "chance encounter" had been planned. Kashi took one look at him and you could watch her melt. Her ears perked up and the light came back into her face. Perhaps she sensed he needed her care, just as Turbo had? It was love at first sight.

Lexington 1993 - 2002

four years old

barbara boswell brunner

The X Games

The two of them destroyed our landscaping in one day, seriously, ONE day. They ran around the yard bouncing off the planting mounds like they were ski moguls. Kashi was happy again. She taught him all of the games she used to play with Turbo and it seemed like life would get back to normal. As Lexington grew, though, we noticed he was having trouble with stamina. He would play in short bursts but then need to rest.

An orthopedic vet confirmed our suspicion later that month. Lexington's dysplasia was getting worse as he grew. His hip sockets were almost flat. We had a choice of a full hip replacement with titanium hips, or remodeling each hip joint. Either surgery would keep him confined to a crate for a year. We had to wait for him to become full grown before we could make any decision, so we had time. We knew it was best to keep his weight down as much as we could and let him dictate his own play schedule. He learned to hop with his back legs together instead of a normal gait and could really get up some speed. Perhaps something he had learned from his lop-eared bunny buddy?

I was opening my fifth shop in Portland, Oregon. We had leased a 7000 square foot space for Dakota's new flagship store. It needed a good deal of remodeling before it would be ready to open and Ray and I decided to stay in Portland for two months to work directly with the contractor. Of course we took the dogs with us. We stayed at a very nice hotel in downtown Portland who welcomed our dogs with open arms, on one stipulation. We could not take them in the guest elevator to and from our third-floor room. We had to use the stairs. That was OK with us. We liked taking the stairs and it was good exercise.

After a week, the stairs began to take a toll on Lexington's hips. He couldn't take the pain anymore and cried every time we started up or down. For the next seven weeks, Ray carried him up and down those stairs, fifty pounds of puppy— and some days he carried him eight blocks to the store. Lexington and Ray had an undeniable bond.

Ray is a very talented designer as well as businessman and with the help of our contractor Ted and his co-worker, artist Karen McClain, the four of us were able to get the remodeling done on schedule. Ted and his crew, along with Ray, built and installed fixtures and Karen painted and installed our trademark wall quotes. Yes, we were doing that long before the rest of the retail world caught on...I worked on the inventory receipt, staff hiring and operations. All while the dogs played and napped.

I am sure they thought this new "house" they were in was pretty strange, but they adapted. The shop was built on two levels with a large circular ramp decorated with a two-story mural replica of Tamara de Lempika's "Adam and Eve." The dogs developed a game where they raced to the top of the ramp, took a running start and slid back down. They were comical. Kashi could turn ANYTHING into a toy or a game.

We were so tired at the end of most days that all we could do for dinner was order room service. Caesar salad became our staple and we quickly discovered it was Lexington's favorite, too. He had never been a beggar, but he could not resist that salad. If we turned our backs for a second, our salads would be gone.

We also discovered on that trip that he loved jalapeño peppers—two very odd things for a dog to love.

He continued to surprise us with odd likes over the years including his love of golf. He would sit for hours and watch golf on TV. He watched the tournament, not listened to it. It was as though he understood the game. When the commercials came on, he did what all men do, used the facilities and got a drink then returned to his chair to watch the tournament. If he ever had to stay alone for any period of time we turned on the Golf Channel to keep him company.

One of the items we sold in my shops was handmade soap. I had just finished putting a display together and it looked beautiful—freshly sliced bars of soap arranged on silver trays surrounded by lemon grass stalks. Ray and I left for a meeting leaving Karen alone in the shop with the dogs. Lexington and his odd likes...He grabbed a slice of lemongrass soap and started eating it. Karen was mildly terrified of large dogs but she knew this would make him really, really sick. Multiple commands were given to drop the soap and Lexington was not listening. Finally she gathered all of her confidence, reached into his large mouth and extracted the soap. Yea Karen! And she still had all of her very well insured fingers intact. Whew!

The shop opened to rave reviews and we went home to Redmond. It was time to decide what to do about Lexington's hips. He was now almost full grown. Dr. Randy was skeptical about surgery. He had been researching it extensively while we were in Portland and he was not convinced it would work. Lexington's hip sockets and balls were almost completely flat. The remodeling surgery was definitely not an option anymore and new hips were going to be a bigger challenge than we thought. Because the ball on his leg bone was flat he would need it rebuilt as well as need a full set of titanium hips.

Dr. Randy was not recommending the surgery. He wanted to try Lexi on a new drug called Rimadyl, an anti-inflammatory, to see how he managed. He was interested in giving Lexington the best quality of life possible and keeping him in a crate for a year was just not a good option for either of the dogs. We agreed and found that Rimadyl worked very well to manage his pain. It would become a daily routine, but was a better solution than surgery. He suffered no ill effects; his blood work returning normal after every test.

We were lucky. Most dogs do not tolerate Rimadyl on a long term basis. It can cause stomach and intestinal upset as well as kidney failure. It provided Lexi enough pain relief that he could start accompanying us on short walks. We knew if he built up strength in his leg muscles they would help support his hips. Kashi helped the most, though, with her games. She kept him running throughout the day. She played with him hard and then would let him rest. She had it all figured out and seemed to instinctively know how far to push him. She became his personal trainer. She also taught him the same mouth-wrestling game she had played with Turbo as he got too ill for any other games. When they played it we always felt like a little piece of Turbo was still with us.

Wall? What Wall?

The months passed. Kashi and Lexington fell into a good routine in the Redmond house. They had a fenced yard, a dog door, and lots of room to play. When spring came around, Lexington discovered a tasty treat in our Japanese maple trees. It started with a couple of leaves being plucked off. We laughed and thought it was just another quirky thing he liked to eat until we came home from the office one day to find every tree stripped bare. He had delicately plucked every single leaf and eaten it. The branches were all perfectly intact and the trees looked as though it were the middle of winter. We spent that summer looking at bare trees. Every time a leaf would begin to sprout he was right there ready to enjoy it. He must have thought it was the coolest doggie vending machine, dispensing sugar-filled greenery. YUM!

Children were fascinated with Lexington. He had a very sweet face with silver dollar sized, rust colored eyebrows that could melt anyone's heart. They would run right up to him, hug him and say "Carl, I love you." We were not at all familiar with the Carl books and had to read one to see what it was about. "Good Dog Carl" is a book series written by Alexandra Day, a Pacific Northwest author, about her Rottweiler Carl. Carl has many adventures and the books are used in many Seattle area schools. Lexi did look quite a bit like Carl and we loved when he would make kids smile. Parents were often intimidated by him but their kids were not.

We always encouraged the kids to ask before they would pet him or hug him letting them know they should never just run up to a dog and touch it. Not all dogs are as friendly as Carl and Lexington, we warned. Lexi seemed to communicate well with the kids and I have always looked back on that experience and wondered how much he would have enjoyed being a therapy dog in a children's hospital. We should have taken the time to get him certified. He would have been a wonderful companion for sick kids. Rottweilers are a very gentle breed, protective of their families, thoughtful and kind. Their bad reputation is undeserved and is only a result of bad owners. I learned to regret my words from the pet shop. He was as far from a baby killer as you could get. If he was told it was his job, I know he would have given up his own life to protect that of a child.

Lexington did have days of boredom that led to lots of puppy mischief. It was frequently rainy and cold in Redmond and he couldn't easily play outside. It made his hips hurt. Kashi was getting into her middle age years and liked to sleep in front of a warm heat vent. If he couldn't get Kashi to play with him what was he to do? We found out the day we came home to a hole he had chewed through the entry hall wall into a bathroom cabinet. The studs in the wall were also missing as was the side of the cabinet. He had eaten right through them. A hole just big enough for that big fat Rottie head to fit through. A week or so later he destroyed the bottom step of our staircase. Yep—also missing. Thankfully our days in Redmond were coming to a close and Lexington would get a chance to break his chewing habits in a new home.

barbara boswell brunner

FIRE!!

Ray had a friend who purchased a boot company in Nashville and asked Ray to come and help run it. Instead of selling our home, we gave it to our daughter Kristin and her Rottweiler, Bronte. They lived there happily for many years with Bronte being her protector.

One night while Kristin was entertaining her friends with a dinner party, Bronte started barking wildly, running in and out of the house. Kris and her friends did not pay attention initially. Bronte did not give up and finally convinced one of the guys to follow her outside.

The air was filled with smoke and he felt heat on his face. Flames were shooting through the roof and windows of the home next door, only a hundred feet away. Bronte had given them the warning they needed to call the fire department and save her home. Good Dog Bronte!

barbara boswell brunner

Crazy Town, USA

Living in Nashville was a hoot, literally and figuratively. We had an enormous white owl that lived in a tree by our driveway. Lexington was always fascinated by the sound the owl would make and lay at the base of the tree for hours, watching it. The sound seemed to calm him on a rough day. In Nashville there were plenty of those. It was a city we lived in for just a few years, but came out with enough stories to be the headliner entertainment at cocktail parties for many years to come. There were the massive thunderstorms, tornadoes, lightening strikes, kidnappers, the bank robber, the SWAT team helicopter, Yabba Dabba Do, the home invasion, the car wreck. Oh, the list goes on and on.

Our garbage collectors adored Lexington. They knew he was generally outside in the yard and would always bring him treats. He would launch himself like a rocket through the yard to greet them. They played a not-very-funny trick on a new trainee one day asking him to walk down our driveway alone to get the garbage can. They stood on the street howling with laughter as Lexington raced to get his treat, causing major panic in the poor trainee. He screamed "KILLER DOG," jumped into the trash can for protection and wet his pants. I watched this from my office window and could not help but feel sorry for the guy. He was so embarrassed when Lexi reached up and licked his hand.

Lexington, three years old

Ear Protection Gear Required...

Kashi was getting older. She was now fifteen and just starting to show her age. We knew we wouldn't have her too much longer. Dobermans generally do not live past ten or twelve and we looked at every day as borrowed time. A puppy for her to train would be ideal! I was at the market one afternoon and sitting by the front door was a woman with a cardboard box. Inside the box was the cutest puppy I had ever seen, albeit one who was being terribly vocal. I was quite surprised that a sound that loud could come from such a tiny being. She was not old enough for it to be a bark; it was a sonic squeal of puppy excitement. It was, however, a hint of things to come...

I am not one who can walk by a puppy, especially one this adorable, so I stopped to pat the puppy's head and talk to the woman to find out her story. She and her husband were the owners of a purebred Dalmatian who accidentally had relations with the neighborhood-roving Black Lab resulting in a litter of nine puppies. All had been given away except for this one. Despite the non-stop vocalization, she was irresistible. As soon as I picked her up she stopped the eardrum shattering noise and started giving me kisses and cuddled against my chest. She was soft, warm and fit nicely in the palm of my hand. Her fur was the softest I had ever felt, like warm velvet. I understood why Cruella Deville wanted to make coats in 100 and 1 Dalmatians. She was too small to climb from the foot well of my Jeep to the seat. Madison, as we would name her, was all Labrador Retriever from the aerial view and black as night. Her underbody from chin to the tip of her tail was white with tiny black spots and all Dalmatian. When showing her to anyone new, I would hold her in one hand (Lab); flip her to the other hand (Dalmatian). She still had intoxicating puppy breath. Ahhhh.

I arrived home with my little furry acquisition. Ray was out in the "back-forty" cutting down trees. Our home nestled in the middle of ten wooded acres and we were clearing brush, making room for a pool and our own jogging trail. Kashi and Lexington were with him and as I approached with this tiny puppy, he thought I had found a baby skunk in the yard. The dogs came bounding toward me and Ray yelled "Kashi, Lexi... NOOOOOO!!" I think he was having Post Traumatic Stress Disorder from our San Francisco skunk experience. As I got closer he realized it was a puppy, not a skunk, and couldn't wait to cuddle and get puppy kisses. It had been a long time since he had smelled puppy breath. Madison learned quickly how to con her dad. All it took was a snuggle, a wag of the tail and a kiss.

Lexington was immediately as smitten as Ray and I were. Kashi could not have cared less. She threw her head up in the air and huffed away. Well, that's a good sign, I thought. At least this one is healthy! We headed back up to the house with Madison bounding alongside Lexi. Wherever he went, she was not far behind. He was a good caretaker for her. He taught her the ropes, taught her about the Invisible Fence, and where she could and couldn't go. When he lay down to take a nap she was always tucked in between his legs snuggled up against his warm belly.

We were having a new multi-level deck built onto the back of our house. Because of the land slope, the deck was suspended two stories high. On the day I brought Madison home, the stairs and railings to the lower levels had not yet been installed. We watched her for an hour looking at the edge of the deck. No...no way would she try to jump, we thought. She walked up close to the edge to investigate, we would say "careful," our danger word for the Invisible Fence. She would then walk back to the safety of Lexington's legs. Good sign we thought. She's already figured out a boundary. HA! Were we wrong...? We gasped as she charged full speed toward the edge and took a swan dive, legs fully extended like a flying squirrel, SPLAT onto the stones below. We ran to the edge expecting to see a very damaged puppy and there she was...running down into the back-forty at full speed. Not a scratch on her.

Crate training seemed like a necessity for this one. We had never done it before but read lots of books and information. It seemed like the way to go with a pup this energetic. Kashi and Lexington were finally broken of their habit of sleeping in our bed and had nice wicker basket beds on the floor. I wanted to start this little girl out right. We liked having the bed back to ourselves.

Night one of crate training—Madison turned into a screeching banshee. We did everything the books said. We ignored her and tried to get some sleep. Eventually the crate got moved to the opposite side of the house. Ray could still not ignore her. Her cries were piercing and I was sure the neighbors thought we were doing her great bodily harm. At one point Ray mentioned something about flushing her down the toilet if she didn't shut up.

Midnight...screeching...

1:00 AM....screeching...

2:00 AM....screeching...

At 3:00 AM, Madison was taken out of the crate and tucked in nicely at the foot of our bed, peacefully sleeping, and that is where she slept for the remainder of her life. Crate training...major fail.

Madison, six weeks old

Madison 1995 – 2010

fifteen years old

Neener, Neener, Neener

The first couple of months with Madison were mostly uneventful. She spent time growing and learning her commands. She really got the commands down quickly. "Leave it," meant put it immediately in your mouth and chew. "Come," meant turn and run as fast as you can in the opposite direction from which the command originated. "Sit and stay," meant dance around like a clown. She would look at the person delivering the command with a defiant, yet impish look. It's not that she didn't understand; she knew perfectly well what you wanted her to do. She was just an independent little—well, you get the idea. Madison had many professional trainers work with her over the years and all but one said the same thing. She was too smart for her own good, very confident, extremely stubborn and un-trainable unless she CHOSE to be trained.

We signed her up for puppy kindergarten, a month of day care and training. I took her every morning and dropped her off and picked her up in the afternoon. At the end of the second week the owner took me aside and asked me to not bring her back. She was disruptive to the class and showed no hope of getting trained. She stole the other puppy's toys, wouldn't rest at naptime and insisted on giving puppy kisses when being shown a new command instead of listening. It was too much for them to handle.

An article in the newspaper gave us hope. It highlighted a Schutzhund trainer in Nashville. Schutzhund training is a very rigorous process involving training for tracking, obedience and protection. We immediately set her up for a two-week board and train. We didn't want her trained for protection, but knew that this trainer's skill set could relate well to Madison's stubborn temperament. His evaluation of Madison was that she was extremely intelligent and would be a good candidate for his obedience classes. He felt her stubborn nature could be an advantage once she learned what was expected of her. Madison excelled with her training—Come, Sit, Stay, Down, Leave It...all mastered in just two weeks of board and train.

When we picked her up we were introduced to a well-mannered and polite dog, no barking, no crazy running and dancing. The trainer demonstrated each command several times, had us work with her and we had the same results. Wow, we thought. What have you done with Madison? This has to be an imposter. We were so grateful that we had found this dog magician. Then she came home, jumped out of the car, looked back at us defiantly and took off running, straight through her Invisible Fence. As she went running into the wind with a smile on her face we imagined her saying, "neener, neener, neener...you can't catch me." Ahhh, Madison was back.

Madison was absolutely the most ill-mannered dog we ever had and retained that title until the day she passed on, just a few days shy of her sixteenth birthday. She made Marley, from the book Marley & Me look comatose. Kashi ate sofas, five in all. Lexington ate a wall. Turbo ate a chain link fence. But I never knew one dog could get into as much trouble as Madison. She had the nine lives of a cat. She was always into some sort of trouble that should have resulted in her demise. She was hit by a car, thrown 20 feet into the air and 50 feet down the road. I gasped and thought I would be scraping her up off the asphalt. Nope. She bounced up like "whoa...that was FUN!" She was stung on the tongue by a wasp she was trying to play with and an hour later stung by another. She ate a full bottle of Kashi's thyroid medication. She ate an entire row of heather from the garden, which was not particularly good for her digestive system. She was standing right beside a power pole when it was struck by lightning. She regularly jail-broke through her Invisible Fence and took off into traffic and the surrounding neighborhood.

I had a very bad feeling the afternoon I discovered Madison missing. I had been watching her in the yard just moments before and now could not find her anywhere. She was still quite small, maybe only three months old and had not started wandering out of our yard yet. She generally never left Lexington's side, yet there he was, standing in my office door without her; head cocked to one side with one eyebrow arched with concern. The look on his face told me something was wrong. I started to search the yard and then the neighborhood. Madison was nowhere to be found.

I flagged down a UPS truck that was approaching and told the driver my dilemma. The driver, Linda, joined in the search. A mile away in a development across the road from our home there were three ten-year-old girls playing in their front yard. She stopped to inquire if the girls had seen Madison. The girls said no, they had not seen a puppy, when from behind one of them a little black nose appeared. Linda said, "That looks like the puppy I am searching for." The girls vehemently denied any knowledge of a puppy, shoving the dog behind them. Then Linda noticed a red leather collar, just like Madison's, lying on the ground by the road. Asking the girls about it they again denied any knowledge of a puppy or a collar. Linda jumped out of her truck and looked behind the girls where she found little Madison wrapped in a blanket. Suddenly the story changed.

"Oh, THIS puppy?" they exclaimed. "We just found her and she didn't have a collar so we thought we could keep her." When questioned about the collar by the road, the girls offered no explanation. Linda collected Madison and her collar, driving her back to the safety of home.

Later that evening I went to the girl's house at a time I knew the parents would be home and explained the afternoon events. The girls had finally confessed that they were walking home from school, saw Madison in our yard and stole her to keep for themselves. Mom and Dad had told them they could not buy a dog, but if they found one, they could keep it. This was their version of "finding a dog." I thanked them for finally being honest and told them they could always stop on their way home from school to play with her, but they could NEVER take her from the yard again. They agreed and their afternoon stop became something Madison anticipated with copious tail wagging.

I regularly received UPS shipments of product for my shops at our home in Tennessee, so I got to know Linda quite well. As Madison grew she decided that investigating the UPS truck would be something interesting to do and would sometimes hitch a ride. Linda would find Madison in the back of her truck with the packages, chomping happily on Linda's lunch or taking a nap on one of the package shelves. She had to become extra vigilant and keep the truck doors closed when she entered our driveway. Madison was not deterred. She would start running from the far side of the yard, launch herself at the nose of the UPS truck, bounce off the engine compartment and land on the roof. She was going to find a way to get into that truck. Linda sometimes found her sleeping on the roof of the truck many blocks from home. Oh, how easily she could have fallen and been run over in the road. Not our Madison. Perhaps she had the gift of Spiderman skills...

Dogs Cannot Fly

By the time Madison was four or five months old she managed to annoy even Lexington, Mr. Patience of a Saint. He was usually extremely tolerant of her; however, he had his limits. She would not stop hanging off the side of his face. She would latch onto his jowl as he walked, acting like a baby monkey hanging off its momma. He shook his head hard and threw her across the living room smashing her into the wall on the opposite side. The impact left a dent in the drywall. She was unscathed and I know Madison thought it was a Disney E ticket ride—oooh, another oldster reference. Years before Disneyland instituted an all-inclusive fee, you paid by the ride. E Tickets were for the best of the best: rides in high demand that were fast and adrenaline pumping.

barbara boswell brunner

A Flizzard of Epic Proportion

Madison's skill at "the kill" was astonishing. She apparently got a keen hunting talent from her roving-hoodlum puppy-dad. Her prey included turtles, birds, snakes and moles. We were having a terrible problem with moles digging up our yard. We tried mole traps, smoke bombs, and even in-ground battery operated thumpers. We decided that Tennessee moles must wear gas masks and be deaf. Nothing worked until Madison decided one day that moles made a pretty awesome toy. She and Lexington would tag team. Madison would put her nose to the ground sniff them out and then Lexington would dig up the spot and grab them. Then tug of war began. It's gross, but it worked. Within a month all of our mole problems had moved to the neighbor's lawn.

Her "kill" skills also were applied to stuffed animals. They were not safe in our home, EVER. She would attack them, decapitate, gut and pull out the squeaker—every stuffed toy, every time, in less than a minute. She tore them up like she was working against the clock; a contestant on a puppy game show. She was methodical and precise. Once the squeaker was plucked, she spit it out and walked away leaving behind a headless, deflated toy, stuffing strewn everywhere. A sight we called a flizzard.

Air conditioning is a necessity in the South and a unit that is not functioning quickly causes great discomfort. Ours broke down on a ridiculously hot Nashville day and the repairman was on his way. I needed to keep Madison confined so she didn't steal his tools. She was well known with our local tradesmen for her kleptomania. It would not be unusual for us to be gardening and find a screwdriver or a hammer partially buried. This repairman needed access to the kitchen, normally the only safe spot we could keep Madison. I shut her in our bedroom thinking she would fall asleep on the bed.

When I opened the door to let her out, a cloud of white downy clusters greeted me. Not just a few clusters. I could not see into the room. I KNEW she was being too quiet. She had decided it would be great fun to shred the down pillows and down comforter and then, if that were not enough, she threw them around the room like rag dolls. They were her prey du jour. There were little white downy clusters on the ceiling, on the walls, in the draperies, in our closet and of course Madison was now white, head to toe, encased in a flizzard of epic proportion. She looked at me with a twinkle in her eye, "That's what you get" silent but implied.

barbara boswell brunner

Houdini in a Dog Suit

At six months old, Madison got her first Invisible Fence collar. It was huge on such a tiny little girl; a box three inches long and two inches square. I think it weighed as much as her head. She had been very good staying by Lexi's side but we knew that would not last forever. My office was in our guest wing and I had a wonderful view of the yard from my windows. I had no hesitation leaving the three dogs free to roam their yard during the day. One day I noticed Madison getting closer and closer to the fence limit and with a twenty-five-foot head start, ran at full speed and jumped at exactly the right moment to jump OVER the fence's radio field. Off she went. By the time I got out to the yard she was gone.

We had a runner.

An hour later I found her at a home almost a mile away, standing in front of the kennels for their hunting dogs. She was trying to break them out. She was her father's daughter. Once a hoodlum, always a hoodlum.

Kennel breaking was a skill Madison would become famous for. When we traveled, we would board the dogs with our veterinarian. In the morning they would arrive and find all of the boarded dogs running loose in the building. This occurred every night and only when Madison boarded. She could open a simple gate latch with her nose. The hoop catches took a little more skill, needing both nose and paws. She figured them all out quickly. She even learned to open a peg latch with a twist bolt. Madison had issues with confinement. They finally had to put a combination lock on her kennel and retired it with fanfare the day we moved away. Their nickname for her was:

"Houdini in a Dog Suit."

Yabba Dabba Dooooo!

There was not a friendlier puppy than Madison. She liked everyone, her thick tail thumping loudly when anyone new came to visit. She was the first to greet and the last to say goodbye. Her cold-nose crotch-greetings were particularly refreshing on a hot summer day with our female friends wearing dresses. She never met anyone she didn't like and everyone liked her back. That is until the day of Yabba Dabba Do.

Ray and I were working in the office with a computer tech trying to fix a glitch with our new computer system. All three dogs were sleeping peacefully under the desks. From the living room I heard a faint "hello?" It seemed rather odd since we were on ten acres, the house was in the middle of the property and we had a two-hundred foot driveway. Ever so curious, I ventured out. In the living room stood a woman wearing a Flintstones Yabba Dabba Do tee shirt, looking a bit confused. I asked if I could help her.

She proceeded, in a VERY heavy southern accent "Yur dawg trayed me." Having absolutely no idea what she was talking about I asked her to repeat it and again "Yur dawg trayed me." She smelled strongly of alcohol and I suspected something was amiss. She began explaining a hair-brained story that I only understood a few words of, so I called my interpreter, Ray. I told him she had a story he just had to hear. He asked how he could help her and got the same answer "Yur dawg trayed me."

Fortunately Ray speaks "southern." He immediately knew this woman was saying our dogs had chased her up a tree. Ah ha. So silly-me asks "Our dogs chased you up a tree?" "Yes ma'am." Yabba was outstandingly polite. "A tree in our yard?" I quizzed "So you were trespassing?" "No ma'am I was across the street," Yabba replies.

Now I was confused. "I don't understand," I said. "The dogs have a fence that keeps them in their yard, how did they chase you up a tree across the street?" "I saw it chasing me and I got scared. I've been up in the tree for hours," Yabba tearfully explained.

At this point Ray took over the conversation with Yabba. "So let me make sure I understand you correctly," he said. "My dogs chased you up a tree across the street, while they were standing in MY yard?" "Yes sir," she declared, confidently. "Did my dog leave the yard while chasing you?" asked Ray. "No sir," mumbles Yabba.

Ray was intrigued. "Which dog?" he asked, thinking maybe she saw a Doberman or Rottweiler in the yard and got scared, a stupid, but definite possibility in someone whose judgment skills are impaired.

"Sir, the MEAN BLACK DOG WITH A TAIL," slurred Yabba.

Now I was (quite impolitely I may add) in full hysterics. Madison, our little Nobel Peace Prize dog, had scared her from five acres away and fearing for her life from the mean black dog with a tail, she climbed a tree. I could not stop laughing and said "If you are so afraid of dogs then why did you walk into our home, without knocking and call out hello? The dogs LIVE here. I can call them; they're just down the hall."

A look of fearful confusion came across Yabba's face. At this point Ray says "Time to go" and starts to escort Yabba to the door. Yabba responds with "You can't treat me like this. I'm gonna call my LAWYER." Ray's amusement was evident on his face. "Honey, I hate to break this to you but I don't think you can even spell Lawyer."

"CAN TOO!" she boasts loudly.

"L , A"...long pause and furrowing of brow...

"DUBAHUUUU"...another long pause,

"no, no, Y...W,E,R."

We were laughing so hard we could barely compose ourselves. Yabba walked up the driveway, muttering to herself, never to be seen again...

Criminals Abound

We had so many unbelievable happenings while living in Nashville. One evening, while Ray was still at work I was watching the news and preparing dinner. Lexington was making an unusual amount of noise barking by the front window. He was rather stoic and only barked if he was really concerned about something. I tried to get him to quiet down. There was a story I wanted to hear on TV. A convicted bank robber had escaped from the Nashville jail. His girlfriend's home was near our neighborhood, and the police suspected he may be headed that way.

Lexington was still barking. As I went out to investigate, I heard the description of the escaped convict; tall white male, long hair, wearing a dark-colored prison jumpsuit and a baseball hat. As I opened the front door to see what Lexi was annoyed with, he bolted past me, knocking me back into the doorway and planted his body between me and whatever it was he found so disturbing. With the Invisible Fence he could go no further so he stayed on the porch barking madly.

I had never before heard him be so convincingly ferocious. I glanced in the direction he was looking and saw...a tall man in dark clothing wearing a baseball cap. He appeared to be trying to break into our Jeep. I yelled and he ran. I called the police who showed up in less than sixty seconds.   They were already patrolling the neighborhood looking for this guy.   The Jeep was dusted for fingerprints and it was confirmed they were from the escaped bank robber. The police searched our property to no avail.

The sky was moonless and it was pitch black.   Our ten acres were surrounded by other ten-acre properties, also heavily wooded.   The police warned us to keep the doors locked and dogs inside; this guy was armed and dangerous. They praised Lexington for his instincts and said if there were any more problems that night, to call them immediately; they would be close by. The rest of the evening was quiet and we retired to bed.

At 5:00 AM the sun had just started to rise. The windows of our second story bedroom looked out over the deep valley of our backyard acreage. Lexington was standing by the window snarling, with a deep resonating snarl, not a growl. He saw something he was unfamiliar with and was trying to warn us. Ray awoke and sleepily asked what the sound was. There was a soft repetitive noise coming from the back forty; whoosh, whoosh, whoosh. We crawled out of bed and stood almost face to face with a black SWAT helicopter hovering over the back yard. On the ground below were SWAT officers in full combat gear, with a man face down on the ground in handcuffs. We were standing in the window, in our pajamas; our jaws on the floor. The convicted bank robber escapee had been hiding out on our property all night. SWAT had discovered him in the early morning hours and waited until sunrise to make the capture.

The woods also provided sanctuary for a kidnapper. With the dogs romping around us one weekend, we worked on the landscaping in the front yard. We were familiar with an abandoned cabin across the street but never saw anyone living in it. That afternoon a car kept driving in and out of the dirt road leading to the cabin and we thought someone must have purchased the property. Oh goodie, new neighbors, we thought. Madison took particular interest in the car and alerted us every time it went in or out the road. Her doggie instincts were keen. On one trip we both noticed a little boy pressing his face against the window of the car making faces. Cute kid, I thought to myself. Maybe he'll come over and introduce himself when they get settled.

The following morning, Madison and I were returning from a trip to the dry cleaners. It was often easier to take her with me on short trips than to face the destruction from leaving her at home. As I approached home, I saw a car parked on our lawn and stopped to see if they needed help. There was a woman yelling at a little boy who appeared to be about ten years old. She explained that she saw him on the side of the road and accused him of truancy.

This very uptight, bee-hive-hairdo'd woman wanted to call the police and get the boy taken to school where he belonged but she did not have a cell phone. I had a phone in my car and called the police. I thought this seemed like a much better idea than watching her put the child in her car and drive away, which is what I feared would inevitably happen.

Shortly, I realized it might be the same little boy I had seen the day before, making faces in the car window. He was crying and said the lady would not listen to him. He needed help. His mother, his sister and he had been kidnapped. They were being held in a cabin across the street. The lady refused to accept the story, told him he had a much too vivid imagination. She continued chastising him for cutting school. Then he looked at me with those big teary eyes and wailed. "Why didn't you help me yesterday? I was begging you to help us!"

Oh my God. He WAS the little boy from the car. Now his faces from the day before made sense. I hugged him and told him the police would be there any minute to help. I got Madison out of the car and she sat by his side to comfort him. He hugged her and told her he knew that she understood what he needed the previous day. Madison licked his face in acknowledgement. They had indeed been kidnapped and this brave little boy managed to escape so he could get help for his mom and sister. Madison stayed by his side until mom and sister were rescued and the kidnapper was in handcuffs. As they towed the kidnapper's Cadillac from the dirt road, I was astonished to see OUR license plate attached to the car. Just another day in Crazy Town...

barbara boswell brunner

Pong

The weather in Nashville would be a challenge on numerous occasions. It was terribly hot in the summer with ice storms and massive snowstorms in the winter. Our woods were home to many bird species, especially during spring migration. Many days we would have thousands of robins resting for the evening on their long spring flight. The spring of 1997 was unusually cold. We were having nighttime temperatures below thirty degrees.

We were enjoying our coffee on a sunny but still unusually chilly Saturday morning. Out of the corner of his eye, Ray noticed something fall from a tree in the front yard and watched Madison run toward it. He wasn't sure what it was so he stared out at the ground for a minute. Thump. Something else fell and again Madison raced to it. As we both started watching the trees there was another thump. A robin had been sitting on a branch and it fell, just like a cartoon bird; then another, then another. Madison was chasing every one as it fell. She looked as though she were playing a game of Pong. (Okay, another "yes I am an ancient reference." This one you'll have to look up for yourself.) Some were hitting her on the head. The birds had been frozen to the branches in the nighttime temperatures and as the morning sun warmed the trees, the birds fell to the ground. She nudged them with her snout and when they didn't move she went off to inspect another.

When we realized what was happening we raced to the yard to see if we could save any of the birds. Sadly we could not. The birds were all frozen. By the end of the day we had picked up and bagged hundreds of birds. It was tragic and we felt helpless. I wanted to knit them all little bird sweaters.

CRACK!

The Tennessee Valley gets enormous thunderstorms and there were days that seemed like the Apocalypse was upon us. Some came with massive rumbling thunder and some spawned tornadoes. Our highest tornado count was fifty-two in a five-hour period in the spring of 1995. Anytime I heard thunder it was never too alarming, as long as tornado warnings had not been issued. If it got loud enough Madison and Lexington would come inside. Neither had any fear of the noise. Kashi, however, was terrified and could always be found hiding in the closet or under a large piece of furniture. Her fireworks experience from San Francisco always haunted her.

One particular day the rumbling had been going on for hours. I mistakenly thought all dogs were accounted for; Kashi was finally asleep at my feet. Lexington was in the hallway. I incorrectly assumed Madison was not too far away from Lexi. At that age she rarely ventured anywhere without him. As the storm grew closer I did a puppy head-count. Madison was unaccounted for. "Uh, oh," I worried.

At almost the same moment, came a blinding light and massive crack of thunder. The utility pole outside my office window had been hit by lightning and five feet away sat Madison, looking a bit stunned. I raced to grab her and carried her inside. Her fur was full of static. The top of the pole was on fire and I could imagine there was not too much time before it either fell or caught the roof on fire. With Madison in one hand and the phone in the other I punched out the number for the fire department. Madison's heart was racing. I reported to the fire department that the pole was on fire and it was possible my dog had been struck by lightning. They arrived in what seemed like an instant, put out the pole fire, checked on Madison and offered to take us to the vet for an exam, but by now Madison was acting like nothing had happened. She had no burns and her fur was not smoldering. She was enjoying all of the activity. Cat life number four... poof...

BEACH!
We Must Get
To a Beach

As Madison aged, she appointed herself as Kashi's guardian. Although Kashi had initially snubbed her, they became good buddies. Madison was her protector, her guard and her nurse. We frequently found them curled up together in Kashi's bed. Madison would wash her face and ears. Kashi was getting very old and feebler by the day. She would wander out into the yard and get lost. Madison's wild and insistent barking always got my attention so I could go on a search and rescue mission.

While still in bed early one morning, we heard Madison barking frantically. Kashi was not in her bed. Quickly throwing on clothes, we ran through the yard toward the barking. There was Kashi. She had gotten so skinny that she had fallen through the space between the stairs and the wall. She was hanging in mid air, legs dangling; her ribcage was the only thing keeping her from smashing to the ground. I grabbed her from below and with brute strength, Ray pulled the piece of decking far enough away that Kashi slipped out into my arms. She was undamaged, but frightened.

Having always been thin, her weight loss had been so slow that it was not overtly noticeable. At fifteen years old, Kashi slept most of the time and was not interacting much with the other dogs or us. We thought it was just old age, but a trip to the vet was warranted. Dr. Mike did his exam and with concern said he found something suspicious on her x-ray. He wanted us to take her to a specialist. Kashi had lung cancer. LUNG CANCER? What dog gets lung cancer? Maybe she really WAS getting royalties from that cereal company and spending it on booze and smokes?

It seemed crazy and was hard for us to grasp. Kashi had just weeks to live, the specialist told us. Her tumor was very advanced. At fifteen it would be cruel to put her through surgery that she might not even survive. The specialist told us to take her home and when we felt it was time to euthanize, give Dr. Mike a call. Oh, how we cried. Losing Kashi was as close to losing a child as we could get. How could we make her last days special and comfortable?

BEACH! She hadn't been to a beach since we left Los Angeles. We needed to get her to a beach. The beaches of the Florida Panhandle were many hours away. It was Thursday. With some quick preparations we were ready to leave Friday morning. Our good friend Michael would house-sit and take care of the dogs. He was so amazed at what we were doing for Kashi. It brought tears to his eyes.

We drove all day and at nightfall pulled into the parking lot of the hotel. Fortunately it was off-season and very quiet. Kashi had slept the entire trip. We knew we would need to carry her to the room. She could barely walk from the kitchen to the bedroom at home. While Ray got the luggage I opened the car door to pick up Kashi. Her head came up from her blanket and she sniffed...BEACH!! Those wobbly legs went into action. She got out of the car on her own, running— RUNNING—directly to the water.

Ray dropped the luggage and we both took off after her. Rounding the corner of the hotel, we found her at the water's edge, snapping at the waves, ankle-deep in the water. She was home! We both felt that if she died right there on the beach, nothing would make her happier. The beach was bathed with moonlight so we walked for a while to let her play in the water. We thought she would bite a few waves and then collapse in an exhausted pile. Nope. We walked for more than a mile with her running the entire way. It was good to see her happy. For the next two days, Kashi ran on the beach, played in the water and acted like a puppy. The salt air was what she needed. The beach gave her energy to fight.

Michael was relieved to see us upon our return. He had grown up in rural Washington State and until moving to Nashville to work with Ray had never lived anywhere else. People in Washington State have very little prejudice toward minorities and Michael, being a black man, had never experienced true prejudice until the weekend he dog sat for us. Apparently, the neighbors became very concerned about a black man staying in our home. He called it his Deliverance Moment, recalling the 1972 movie. He swore he heard banjos in the background...*buda-dada dada dada daaaa, nearr-nearrr-nearr-nearr-nearr-nearr-nearr-nearrrrrrr...*

Kashi lived for almost two more years. At seventeen, she was ready to rest. Seventeen seems like it should have earned her some kind of award, huh? The award or reward was ours for the pleasure of her company for seventeen years.

Ray was in Germany working with a client and I was manning the home front. Kashi had a bad morning and for the first time refused her food. She cried and it was obvious she was in unbearable pain. She paced the floor of my office not being able to get comfortable. She whimpered and occasionally let out a scream. By noon I knew it was time to say goodbye. I didn't want to do it without Ray there, but I knew it was time. I hugged her and picked her up. We rocked on the porch swing for an hour and I talked to her about all of the fun things we had done in her seventeen years. She seemed comfortable but still let out an occasional whimper.

Should I call Ray and tell him or not? I was torn. If I did I knew he would leave his meeting immediately and spend the next day on a ten-hour international flight very, very sad. His meeting was important. I decided to euthanize her without Ray and not tell him until he got home in a few days—a decision I have not been forgiven for to this day. It was the hardest thing I had ever done. It wasn't fair that he didn't get to say goodbye but it also wasn't fair for her to live a few more days in excruciating pain.

I wrapped Kashi up, called Dr. Mike and told him it was time. He placed a warm blanket on the cold stainless table to make her more comfortable. I held her paw, kissed her, told her to tell Turbo we missed him. She slipped away. The immense sorrow we felt lasted for a long time.

I picked up Kashi's ashes from the vet on Saturday and placed the brown cardboard box in the trunk of our car. Sunday morning Ray had an early meeting and asked me to go along. We would go to brunch afterwards. Ray drove down the highway, our car in the center lane. We had a car slightly behind us in the high-speed lane and a semi truck slightly ahead of us in the slow lane. We were lined up, but staggered.

Two cars full of teenagers decided it was a great morning for drag racing but when they reached our vehicles, we were blocking their race. One car decided to solve the problem by passing the car in the high-speed lane on the left, in the center breakdown lane, at 115 mph. As he tried to re-enter the high-speed lane, his tires caught the edge of the road, he lost control, slamming him into our car, into the middle of the driver's door. The impact pushed our car to the right, sliding us under the tractor-trailer, in between the front and rear tires. I looked up from my window and all I could see was a set of double truck tires getting closer and closer to my face, the snow chains slamming against the side of the car.

The car that hit us turned perpendicular to traffic, up on two tires and slid sideways down the highway; still going faster than any of the other vehicles. They slammed into the center Jersey barrier and came to a rest with a loud thud, back on all four tires. Ray muscled our car back under control, out from under the semi and was able to pull off to the side of the road. Our car was totaled. The car that hit us was totaled. No one was even slightly hurt—not a scratch. As the tow truck loaded our car, I remembered Kashi's ashes were still in the trunk. I would like to think that she was watching over us that day, keeping us safe.

Kashi, fifteen years old

Her last beach trip— Destin, FL

barbara boswell brunner

White Dog...
There's a SQUIRRELL!!

Madison was like the Welcome Wagon Committee for Nashville. She invited every loose dog in our area home to play with her. It was not unusual for me to walk through the living room in the middle of the day and see Madison sleeping or playing with an unfamiliar dog. We had a Beagle, a Poodle, a yellow Lab, some kind of strange looking mongrel and a Spaniel. The Spaniel came around more than the others, so often in fact, that I felt a need to name him and started calling him White Dog. He had a very worn out leather collar but no tags. The collar was quite constrictive and I had to loosen it up a few notches to make him more comfortable. He appeared very grateful. I felt bad for him. Whoever he belonged to did not take care of him very well. He started showing up every morning on our back deck. Madison would charge out the dog door to greet him and they would spend the day playing in the back-forty. He taught her to catch turtles in the creek and challenge squirrels to staring contests. They were pals. Keeping up with Madison was getting hard for Lexington, so this was a perfect situation. White Dog came every morning and left every evening around dinnertime. I started putting out small bowls of food for him, which he ate hungrily. He was so skinny.

Thanksgiving arrived and Ray and I made plans to travel back to Seattle to visit our daughter for the holiday. We arranged for Lexington and Madison to board at Dr. Mike's office. We were torn about what to do with White Dog. He was with us every day and had been for months but he left every evening. He must have a home that he goes back to, we thought, and it would not be right for us to take him and board him with our dogs. He didn't belong to us.

Upon our return from holiday, Nashville had gotten bitterly cold. It was raining but it felt cold enough to snow. We picked up the dogs from the vet and they were so happy to see us. A week was a long time to be away from them. We lit a fire in the living room fireplace and prepared dinner. Madison kept running in and out of the dog door, even though it was raining hard. As soon as I dried her off she was out the door again. I got her inside one last time and shut the dog door.

I had enough wet dog drying for one night.

Madison was frustrated and we could see it. There was something she needed to tell us. She paced and whined finally ending up in front of the living room windows that flanked the stone fireplace. I looked out to see what in the world had her so bothered. In the corner, between the window and the fireplace sat White Dog; soaking wet, shivering and looking very frightened. Ray scooped him up and dried him off in the laundry room. He was a mess. His fur was filthy and matted and he smelled very bad. He had feces stuck to his fur.

"That's it," I declared. He's staying here tonight.

We gave him a bath and cut the mats out of his fur. He was skin and bones and looked like a concentration camp survivor. After giving him a hearty meal, we put a blanket on the floor by our bed and he curled up and slept. He knew he was finally safe.

White Dog got into a regular routine with us. He decided although he was a true outdoorsman, the house thing was a nice treat. He learned to use the dog door and came and went as he pleased, never leaving our property. We did not put an Invisible

Fence collar on him—he just followed what the other dogs did. If Madison escaped (which she was doing now on a regular basis) he would come get me and take me to the point of her escape. He accompanied me on the search to find her and with his keen scenting skills it usually only took a few minutes to find her. He fit into the family well, giving Lexington the respect he deserved as leader of the pack and becoming my constant companion. He was wise beyond his years. He seemed so grateful to have a home. He spent every night in his own bed on the floor beside me.

One afternoon I observed him stalking a squirrel that was trying to run down a tree. White Dog sat perfectly still, like a statue, for hours. That squirrel would come down a few feet and wait, then a few feet more. White Dog never flinched, sitting a solid as a boulder. He was going to get that squirrel. White Dog almost had him in his reach when, from across the yard Madison came bounding. She was barking crazily and I am sure was saying White Dog, White Dog THERE'S A SQUIRREL!! The squirrel was gone and his fun for the day had abruptly ended. From the look on his face as he hung his head, White Dog was disgusted.

White Dog, Super Augustus, Gus

1993 – 2008

three years old

barbara boswell brunner

I Can Make It To That Door In Two Seconds Flat... Can You?

After White Dog had been living with us full time for over two months, a car pulled into our driveway. A man got out, grabbed White Dog, put a rope around his neck and started dragging him to his car. I ran out in a panic.

What are you doing? You can't take my dog!!" His response was "Hey Lady, he's my dog. Look at his collar I've got his name written on it." "His name is Gus."

The collar came off and of course there was nothing written on it but he seemed convinced that White Dog belonged to him and the dog did respond to the name Gus.

He said without any hesitation, "We remembered we hadn't fed him in a while and thought I better go lookin' for him."

WHAT?? White Dog had been with us for TWO MONTHS and they just remembered they hadn't fed him in a while! Who were these people? As we talked I discovered that Gus, or Super Augustus to the American Kennel Club, was a Brittany from champion stock. He was a wedding present to these folks. I'll call them Dick and Jane to keep them anonymous. Jane didn't like Gus and when they had a baby Gus was relegated to an outdoor kennel. This kennel as we came to learn had no doghouse, no shade and was just a concrete pad with a chain link fence. Good Grief! This was Nashville. The temperature reaches a hundred five degrees in the summer and twenty in the winter. He had no protection from the elements. Gus had learned to escape from the chain link fence to hunt for food and water, then out of loyalty always returned home at night. Dick worked for the IRS. Jane was a surgeon. These were educated people. It was disgusting.

I told Dick that we had really come to love White Dog and would be happy to keep him if he was too much trouble for them. He said no, he really loved Gus too, but thanked me for the offer. I was in tears and ran inside to call Ray. "They took White Dog!" I wailed. I recounted the story to Ray and he said as any rational businessman would, "Call them and start offering them money. At some point they'll say yes."

That's exactly what I did. I found their phone number and called. Jane answered. Before I could even get the words out of my mouth that we would buy him she said, "If you want him we'll bring him right over. He's yours." Five minutes passed and they drove down the driveway. As Dick opened the car door, Gus took off like a shot, directly to the dog door on the opposite side of the house. He was sitting in the entry hall before Dick and Jane even got to the front door. He was home. I asked if they had his veterinary records and they said there were none. Gus had never been to a vet. They told us he now belonged to us and if there was anything wrong with his health they didn't want to know about it. Ironically they also brought an unopened bag of dog food. We still can't pass by the bags of Ole Roy at Wal-Mart without chuckling and remembering Gus. Dick and Jane signed his AKC registration papers over to us and now Super Augustus was ours.

He was three years old.

His first trip to the vet came the following day. He got his first check up, received vaccinations and had a heartworm test. The vet said he seemed to be in relatively good health, despite the neglect he had been through. The heartworm test would be the final bit of information he needed. Heartworm is a parasitic roundworm passed to dogs from mosquito bites. The parasite is commonly called "heartworm;" however, that is a misnomer. The adult worm actually resides in the veins of the lung causing damage to the lung vessels and tissue. Heartworm infection may result in serious disease, including death.

Later that day Dr. Mike called with sad news. Gus had heartworm. He told us that with the heartworm as advanced as it was, Gus would be dead within a year if left untreated. With the treatment he could also die but he could potentially live a full and long life. We chose option two. Gus received his medicine and stayed with Dr. Mike for two weeks. When we brought him home he was a bit plumper and very happy to see us. His little tail was wagging so hard I thought he was going to take off and fly. His treatment went as well as it possibly could and with a little rest, Gus would be good as new. Relief! We had really come to love this guy and had so much admiration for his will to survive.

Dick came back to see Gus one more time before we moved, during an open house. He asked if he could say good-bye to Gus. Ray took him to the basement where the dogs were housed for the day, entering from the outside door. Gus took one look at Dick and bolted through Ray's legs, running to the back of the property. He sat as far away from Dick as he could get. Gus didn't come back inside until Dick was gone. Ray had to go out to retrieve him and assure him he was safe.

Gus, four years old

barbara boswell brunner

The Robbery

On a bright sunny Sunday afternoon in Nashville, Ray's cell phone died. It had been coming for a while. Cell phones back in the dark ages had a very limited life span. On our way to the phone store we passed a pet shop; one of those awful puppy mill pet shops. Of course I had to stop and look at the puppies. Even in their horrible conditions, I couldn't resist. Puppies attract me like moths to a flame. I know it will not end well, but I cannot control myself. "I'll just look" is a phrase I am famous for and why we have adopted nine dogs over the years.

In a small cage in the corner was a tiny little Rottweiler puppy with what looked like a hole in her head. She had ringworm and some sort of awful bronchial infection—probably from living in a filthy cage in a puppy mill pet store. The pet shop workers said she was in isolation and was going to be put down. The owner did not want to pay her medical bills. ARRGGH! That's all I needed to hear. We said we would take her. They actually asked us to purchase her—the nerve! Of course we did pay and rushed her out of the store immediately to Dr. Mike. He gave us medicine for her issues and a bill for less than $100. She was going to be put to death for less than $100. She was completely healthy in a month. Ray never did get a new phone that day and we challenged the credit card charge from the puppy store and won. Within a year the puppy store was closed.

Sutton 1997 – 2004

four months old

The Big Face Girl

Naming her was easy. We were still on our streets of New York naming streak and had a friend on Sutton Place. The name Sutton fit her perfectly. She was adorable—a little ball of fur just ten weeks old. Sutton had Shy Di eyes. She would look at you when caught doing something wrong, holding her head low, but looking up just like Princess Diana. It was sweet. She was very cute, but had a really big face, REALLY big and we nicknamed her the Big Face Girl. We knew she would someday grow into it, but as a puppy it was hilarious. She grew one body part at a time; first her ears, then her face. The rest of her head, her feet, her body and legs all caught up to each other in stages. Her growth spurts were never in sync. We took lots and lots of photos of her so we could always remember how funny she looked as a baby. Sadly, I was slow getting the film developed and we lost it, along with the camera, in The Robbery.

I was in New York on business. Ray was at his office in Nashville. Our home was for sale, with a sign posted in the front yard. Our real estate agent, Bobby, made an appointment that day to show the home to prospective buyers. He asked Ray to leave the alarm system turned off and to put the dogs in the basement. This was something we had done with Bobby many times and Ray did not hesitate knowing he would lock up thoroughly when he left. Ray placed Lexington, Gus and Madison in the basement and put Sutton in her crate in the laundry room. He also placed a sign on the basement door "Three BIG dogs in the basement. Do not open this door." In retrospect, how convenient for the burglars and what probably saved the dogs from being shot and killed. They would have defended their home to the death. The prospective buyers never showed up for their appointment. Bobby called Ray to let him know the prospects were a no show, locked up and left.

Ray decided sometime in the afternoon that he should go home early to let the dogs out. He had an odd feeling when he found out the appointment had been canceled. I swear that man is physic. When he pulled down the driveway he noticed the double doors on the front porch were open and the screen door was propped. Strange, he thought. Maybe

Bobby was still here? Then he realized there were no cars in the driveway. It all registered in his head in an instant—we had been robbed. The double doors had been smashed in with some sort of battering ram that left green paint on what was left of the splintered white double doors. He was inside in a flash and found most of our belongings GONE.

The house was trashed. What they couldn't carry or didn't want, they broke. Mattresses were flipped, closet contents were strewn on the floor, dresser drawers were turned upside down, and my office was in ruins. Where cable lines had been connected to computers and televisions, they yanked the lines out of the wall leaving drywall, desks and bookcases strewn in their wake.

After the initial shock, Ray's first thought was THE DOGS! He raced to the basement door. Were they alive or dead? He was breathing heavily from adrenaline but heard barking. That was a good sign. He opened the door and called them. They came running up the stairs to greet him and were clearly agitated, racing around the hallway with their noses to the ground. Ray must have missed the burglars by minutes. Then his thoughts turned to Sutton. Oh my God he thought; did they steal her too? She was alone in her crate on the opposite side of the house in the laundry room.

With the dogs at his heels, Ray ran across the house, through the guest wing, through the living room, through the kitchen...everyone avoiding the massive amounts of broken objects. Sutton was in her crate but her crate was in the kitchen. They had moved her!

After the police investigation was complete, it was determined that Ray had interrupted the burglary. The screen door had been propped open as a signal. The burglars had another truckload of things to get and that probably included Sutton and our safe, which was pulled out and placed in the middle of the media room. There was a burglary ring targeting homes for sale. They were well organized. Our neighbor, our idiot-neighbor the high school principal, said later, "Oh yea. I saw guys carrying stuff out of the house all day. I thought you were giving stuff away." To me, that explains a lot about the Nashville school system. The only things we lost that could not be replaced were Sutton's puppy photos on the camera and my grandmother's soup tureen. The police dusted for fingerprints but no suspects were ever identified.

After the burglary, Sutton was never the same. The burglars must have terrorized her. Prior to the burglary she loved everyone, was very friendly and social. Now she was wary of any stranger, especially if they raised their voice at Ray or me. Anytime she saw someone wearing a baseball cap or carrying a backpack she went ballistic. We had to be so careful with our friends when they came to visit and remind them to remove their caps around her. Even if she knew the person— no baseball caps allowed.

Michael came to visit one afternoon after Sutton was full grown. He and Sutton had always been buddies. He had just returned from a run and was wearing a baseball cap. Sutton charged at him, snarling and growling. We screamed "Michael, TAKE OFF THE CAP!" just as Sutton lunged at him. He deflected her with his hip, threw his cap to the ground, rolled into a ball and froze. As soon as the cap was on the ground she started wagging her tail and licked him. It is so sad that her life had this one defining moment and it was terror.

barbara boswell brunner

The Graham Technique

One of the sweetest things about Sutton was the affection she demonstrated to us on a daily basis. Like a typical Rottweiler, she was sweet and smart. Unlike most Rottweilers, she was not a stoic dog. She was very expressive, letting you know exactly what she was thinking and what she wanted. She was extremely affectionate and wanted to be held, a lot. She would leap up into our arms and wrap her paws around our neck and waist with no warning. Getting dressed in the morning was a challenge. One of us would walk by the bed and without warning, she would leap into our arms, legs stretched forward like a modern dancer. This caused us to wonder if there were such a thing as a former life, were Sutton and Martha Graham acquainted? If we let her, she would stay like that and allow us to carry her everywhere. She looked like a Koala Bear. It was adorable, but we were glad it stopped as she grew to adulthood.

barbara boswell brunner

2353.6 Miles To Portland

Moving Day arrived. We decided Portland, Oregon, would be our next home. My flagship store was there and Ray had been doing quite a bit of international work for a company who had an office in Portland. It made sense. We found a great 1950's modern ranch house in Portland's West Hills. We had views of downtown, Mt. Adams and the Washington Park Zoo. When the house was built it also had a great view of Mt. St. Helens and Mt. Hood. Tree growth took the view of Mt. Hood and the 1980 volcanic explosion took the top off of St. Helens lowering it out of sight.

We had a dog run built around a third of the house with a dog door attached. Since it got cold and rained quite a bit, the run was all under roof. Although an adjustment from the big Nashville yard, it would be plenty of room for the kids to get fresh air and do their business.

As the moving truck pulled out of our Tennessee driveway, we loaded everyone into the Jeep for the four-day trip to Oregon. With four dogs now, this would not be a sightseeing trip. Lexington and Gus were both three, Madison was almost two and Sutton was six months old. We had quite a brood. Sutton sat on the passenger's lap and the other three shared the back seat. Ray and I took turns driving. We wanted to get there as fast as possible. The trip was fairly uneventful, with the exception of the Kansas diner that Madison decided to bolt from. We stopped for lunch and took the dogs out for their potty break. I didn't close the door quickly enough and Houdini in a Dog Suit had been confined too long. Madison was off like a shot, running directly toward the freeway. My heart skipped a beat.

We screamed, "STOP" and "Madison, COME" to no avail. Her selective hearing took control and I am sure she never even heard us or she just did not care. She was free...

Other travelers in the parking lot saw our dilemma and raced to our aid. We were able to do a good old-fashioned doggie roundup and finally got her back in the car. She was tethered for the remainder of the trip. Bad, bad, Madison.

Arriving in Portland the week after Christmas was fun. The air was crisp and clean. The dogs loved their dog door and dog run. They also loved the back yard, which was completely fenced and backed up to twenty-two undeveloped acres in a land trust. Once our furniture arrived, the dogs were all happily getting settled as Ray and I unpacked boxes.

The weather report was ominous. An ice storm was predicted for that night and when we awoke in the morning we had the worst ice storm in Portland's history; three inches of solid ice. Branches from the trees surrounding the house were snapping and crackling, entire 100-foot trees were falling. One tree fell on the neighbor's roof; one across our driveway. A house down the street was cut in two by a huge fir tree. Our neighborhood looked like a war zone. Then the power went out for a week. Ray had one of the few chain saws in the neighborhood and that kept him busy. The dogs had to learn to ice skate to use their dog run until we could find a tool to chip away the ice. We camped in the lower level family room, which was partially underground and with its wood burning fireplace stayed nice and warm. We were fortunate to have three fireplaces and burned them constantly for a week to keep the house from freezing;

the temperature was in the teens. We cooked on the barbeque grill and had fun. We all piled into the bed in the lower level bedroom at night and snuggled together watching the battery operated TV from our earthquake/tornado/ice storm kit. What a welcome to our new city!

During the ice storm we noticed a cat sheltering in the window-well for the basement. The well had a heavy wooden cover on it that was pushed aside enough for the cat to crawl through, protecting it from the weather above. With the frigid and miserable weather outside, it would not be able to find water or food.

Ray called the real estate agent who assisted with the purchase of the home, who in turn contacted the former owners to see if they were missing a cat. They said yes, it was their cat, but they chose not to take it with them on the move and hoped it would not be any trouble for us. Hello?! We have four dogs!

We discovered that Portland is unfortunately full of feral cats abandoned by owners who either lost interest or could no longer care for them. Although Ray and I are not cat people, we brought the cat inside and put him in a guest room. We could not leave him outside to fend for himself in such bad weather.

We knew none of the dogs would really enjoy a cat, especially Gus, who I am sure in his self-sufficient days enjoyed a tasty feline treat or two. Madison expressed the most interest in Rover, as we called him. She sniffed him, he hissed at her and that was the end of their meeting. Rover got his own room with a litter box and scratching post and stayed warm for the rest of the winter. We eventually found him a great home.

barbara boswell brunner

The Art of Kennel Breaking

Now that we were back in the Pacific Northwest, we needed to take advantage of Academy of Canine Behavior. Madison and Sutton could both benefit from some discipline so we enrolled them in a thirty-day board and train. They had done wonders with our other dogs and we knew they would get Sutton started off on the right foot and Madison, well, we hoped that they could knock some sense back into her. As we stood at the front desk filling out paperwork, a worker came out to take the dogs back to the kennels. We warned them about her ability to escape from almost any kennel enclosure and of her nickname.

"Oh, no worries," they said confidently with typical Pacific Northwest casualness. "Our kennels are very secure."

Sixty seconds passed....All heads snapped to the doorway as Houdini in a Dog Suit came bounding through, like greased-lightning. They were astonished.

During her stay she apparently also shared her escape prowess with the other inmates as she had done in Tennessee. Each morning they found her and other dogs running loose. They called us after a week begging "PLEASE!! Come pick up Madison. We've had enough!"

They couldn't handle her and said she was simply un-trainable. She continuously broke herself and the other dogs out of their kennels and she was barking non-stop. They tried fitting her with a citronella bark-control collar–she ate it within minutes. All she wanted to do was play with the other dogs and had no interest in her trainer. When we got there, her mouth was moving as though she was barking but no sound came out. She had laryngitis.

Academy's conclusion was that she was mentally challenged.... They insisted on giving us a full refund. We knew she was not stupid and in the lobby of the facility practiced the basic commands as taught to us by the trainer in Tennessee. Madison remembered them and performed on command. Sit, Stay, Down, all done perfectly. She was not mentally challenged, just stubborn as a bull and she missed her mom and dad. Her laryngitis lasted for almost a month and the silence was sweet.

Always an angel and willing to please, Sutton stayed at the Academy for the remaining two weeks and passed her course with flying colors.

The dogs settled into their new home and new routine, Ray and I off to work every morning and home for dinner. Depending on what company Ray was working with we would sometimes work together from my shop office. I added an old sofa and brought Madison and Sutton to work with me every day. They had become best buddies and would snuggle on that sofa all day long. If Ray was working out of my office, we would go out for a "date" lunch leaving the two dogs behind, contained by closed double doors. Houdini in a Dog Suit was not a believer in the concept of a closed door. Being left alone, ha! Madison wanted to be with the people.

The doorknob was quickly figured out and off she would sprint to the front door generally with one of my staff members frantically running behind her. She went to the park, she went downtown, and she often found us in the restaurant where we were having lunch. She had no fear of cars and would dash out into the street. If my girls from the shop lost sight of her they only needed to follow the sound of screeching brakes. It finally got to be too much risk and Madison had to stay home. Ray had to padlock the gates to their dog run.

Doughnuts?
What Doughnuts?

Madison did go with me regularly when I drove to Seattle to visit my three northern shops. She was a good travel companion and like Kashi, would rather sit and wait in the car than stay home. On one particular trip I took my personnel manager, Nicki, and merchandising manager, Heather, with me. They wanted to make a fun day of it and thought doughnuts would be a great road trip snack. None of us ate any, but it was a nice thought and I forgot about them. We got out of the car when we reached store number one and walked about a hundred feet from the car when Heather said, "Do you think Madison will be okay with the doughnuts? I left them on the back seat." Oh good grief! I sprinted back to the car and there was Madison, staring back at me with a look of innocence on her face that said "WHAT, Something wrong?" A tiny sliver of doughnut remained hanging from her mouth and the box was empty...

barbara boswell brunner

That's Godzilla, Mom, Not a Dog

Shortly after moving to Portland, friends John and Karen invited us to their home on Lake Oswego. They had two Great Danes, Rama and Sita who were very active and friendly. Madison was getting a little bit of cabin fever missing her big Tennessee yard and we thought it would be a great opportunity for her to run and play with the Danes. After arriving, we got Madison out of the car to introduce her to the Danes. She came into the room, took one look at their size, tucked her tail between her legs and bolted back to the car. She was petrified. It never occurred to us that she would be afraid of anything, let alone a pair of super-friendly dogs.

Two months later, John and Karen came to our home for dinner. As they walked through the door, Madison's nose started sniffing the air. She looked panicked. She tucked her tail and ran for the back yard. Karen knew Madison well and they were buddies. Karen's feelings were hurt until she realized Madison smelled Rama and Sita. Madison had excellent nose memory.

barbara boswell brunner

Bob, Do You Wanna Meet A BIG Dog?

Once a week I would take Lexington to work with me. He liked to hang out with the shop girls and have a change of pace from home. One afternoon Ray and I went out for lunch leaving Lexi in the care of my trusty staff. Denise, a part time associate, had just adopted a new puppy, a beagle named Bob. She brought Bob in to meet Lexington, not realizing we were away from the office. She held Bob out toward Lexi and said, "Bob, do you want to meet a big dog?" Bob squealed, Lexington reached down to pick him up and all that remained were four tiny feet and a faint squeak repeatedly coming from inside Lexi's mouth. *Eepp,eepp,eeeeeeeeeppppppp*!

Denise screamed, the shop girls screamed and Lexington sprinted out of reach, back to my office with Bob. By the time the girls got into the office, there was Lexington, sitting on his bed, grooming a sopping wet puppy like it was the most natural thing for him to do. All of our small stuffed animals with squeakers were thereafter named Bob.

barbara boswell brunner

Sheep-y

Gus became my dog of choice to take to work. He loved it and he knew to stay inside the shop. He got to hang out with the girls on the sales floor and get loved on all day long. If you didn't like dogs you couldn't work for me. Gus did not lack attention. Everyone loved him, brought him treats and visited with him. He was very good for business but business was not good for his waistline. He ballooned from a wispy thirty-five pounds to a whopping seventy-five within a year. It culminated one afternoon when we were having a barbeque at the house and one of our guests used Gus as a table for her beverage. She nicknamed him Sheep-y. His back was perfectly flat and very broad and with his coloring, he did look like a sheep. We realized at that moment we needed to get that weight off of him fast. No more morning bagels and cream cheese for him!

Within a year his weight was down to fifty pounds, but weight would be something he struggled with most of his life. His metabolism had slowed so much from being starved his first three years and it could not adjust to a regular feeding schedule.

His extra weight acted as padding and probably saved his life. We were outside on the deck where Ray was building a new level. It was perched far above the slope on which our home was built. Ray and I were on the new level admiring his handiwork and deciding what type of railing to install. Gus was at our side, looking down over the hill surveying the land. Sutton, who now weighed sixty pounds, came clumsily bounding down the stairs with her big puppy feet and could not stop soon enough. She put on her brakes, but skidded directly into Gus and we gasped as we heard him squeal and watched him plummet off the edge.

"Oh my God," we both screamed and ran to the edge.

Gus had landed thirty-five feet down the hill and was just lying on the ground not moving. The hill was very, very steep and we had to coordinate our efforts to rescue him. I stayed on the deck to direct Ray who had now run back up to the top deck where he had better access to the slope. He grabbed whatever plants he could for a handhold to navigate down the slippery, treacherous hill. Once he reached Gus I was not sure how he was going to carry him.

The hill was muddy from all of the rain we had been getting and Gus was still a little tank of a guy. Ray was twenty feet away when Gus jumped up and started to make his way up the hill on his own. He hadn't broken a single bone, but by that night he had a large and probably painful hematoma on his butt. It was larger than a grapefruit. His extra weight had caused him to fall backwards and land on his hip. A week of painkillers and he was as good as new and never ventured near the edge again. Perhaps Madison let him borrow one of her cat lives.

barbara boswell brunner

Modern, with a little mmmmmmm...

Lexington was the leader of our pack of puppies from the day Kashi died. He was a good leader, strong, silent and benevolent. All of the dogs respected him and never challenged his authority; even Gus, who got special treatment by going to work with me every day. Lexi was not jealous and he and Gus got along like two little old men. He liked to spend his days sleeping and doing his best to stay clear of Madison and Sutton's games. Those two were best buddies and played hard with each other. Our deck and yard allowed them to spend hours running up and down the hills or tearing through the house.

All of the dogs were out of their puppy destructiveness stage and we were comfortable with them having the run of the house during the day. We did not need to worry what mess we would come home to, or so we thought. One afternoon, I arrived home, turned the corner from the kitchen to the living room and there was Sutton... happily chewing on the arm of the sofa.

"*AAAAAAAAAAHHHHHHHHH, STOP!*" I screamed. She acknowledged with a look up of her Princess Diana-like Shy Di eyes seemingly saying, "Hi Mom, what's up. How's your day been...?" She continued chomping on the leather. "Yummm, this is good."

This was no ordinary sofa—it was a black leather Le Corbusier sofa, one of a pair we had purchased many years earlier. Modern enthusiasts know the LC3 for its beautiful lines and rich soft leather, designed in 1929 by Charles Edouard Jeanneret—Le Corbusier—for the Salon d'Automne in Paris. Ray and I have been collectors of authentic modern furniture for many years.

These two sofas were OFF LIMITS to the dogs. It took months to match the leather and find someone to repair it. She also chewed on the corners of an octagonal Frank Lloyd Wright side table we had purchased at a DIFFA auction many years earlier. Our artist friend Karen McClain did an amazing job restoring that piece for us. Sutton had good taste in furniture. I'm also sure she thought it tasted good.

Winning Is Everything

Problems erupted with the girls as Sutton reached puberty. They both weighed sixty pounds. Their games took on a new feeling. They played harder and they seemed to need a winner. Sutton was testing her place in the pack. Our pack order had always been oldest to youngest but that was apparently about to be challenged. We referred to books, to trainers, and the consensus was that they would outgrow it. One would become dominant over the other but in the meantime we should not leave them alone together. Sutton kept pushing and Madison would not back off. They were only a bit more than a year apart in age. It got bloody.

All of our windows were floor-to-ceiling plate glass, the standard for windows in the 1950's and they had never been updated with tempered glass. When we heard the crash, we first thought Madison was just mildly injured until I got her to hold still and realized jagged chunks of glass had slid down the window frame like a guillotine and sliced her across her rump and one thigh, thankfully just missing her spine. There was a large flap of skin and fur dangling from her leg. It was 7:00 AM and we knew the vet's office would not be open. Mild panic set in. What were we going to do?

Always stellar in a crisis, Ray remembered that a week earlier we had seen a placard in a restaurant for the Dove Lewis Emergency Veterinary Clinic in downtown Portland. He even remembered the general address. We wrapped her up in as many towels as we could grab and darted down the hill. Blood was everywhere. Pressure, put pressure on it...was the only thought racing through my mind.

Ray drove like a madman, and with few cars on the road, made it in less than seven minutes. We called ahead so they were prepared for us, meeting us at the car with a stretcher and supplies. Madison was rushed into the clinic. The doctor on call looked at her, made an evaluation and said he felt she would be fine; needing a lot of stitches, but nothing critical had been injured. Whew. We were so relieved. She was resting comfortably but would need to stay there for the day. He would call when it was time to pick her up. Relieved, we went about our day, home to board up the window and clean up the mess.

At noon, the phone rang. It was Dove Lewis. When any conversation starts with "Everything is OK now but..." it usually means something has gone very, very wrong. Another emergency had come in to the clinic just after Madison and it was a more critical situation. Madison's bleeding was sufficiently stopped and it was felt that they could safely attend to the next emergency. While cleaning out Madison's wound, someone missed a piece of glass and it had migrated, cutting a femoral artery. She almost bled out, losing more than half of her blood in a very short time. Fortunately someone was paying attention and caught it in the nick of time. One hundred and fifteen stitches later, Madison came home. Another cat life, gone.

That was not the end of the Madison and Sutton fighting. It seemed to escalate. We were having weekly bloodbaths; blood on the walls, floors and on the ceilings. It was terrible and we felt helpless. On one of our trips to get stitches, a new vet we had not seen before gave us the best piece of advice, ever: Fit them with soft muzzles, put them outside and let them work it out.

One of them would win with no blood getting spilled. It sounded so logical. Why had no one else ever suggested this? Two hours later we had two very tired dogs, no holes to stitch up, and we never had another fight. It was genius! Dr. Ron became our vet for the next ten years.

The Day
The Towers Fell

I wish dogs could talk. It would be fun to have a conversation to hear their perspective. Their thoughts on things they observed could be enlightening. Madison's head would be full of fun games to play. Gus could expound on his days as a stray. Lexington could explain the game of golf, which to this day I do not understand. Hitting a little white ball with a stick....It seems futile.

It would be interesting, but I am glad the dogs do not understand our language. They know when we are upset but they do not know why. They are there to give a comforting lick and say it'll all be ok. However bad it is there are always bones and belly rubs. Kashi was there when my mom died at the young age of fifty-nine, Kashi and Turbo comforted Ray the night his father died. They were with us on birthdays and anniversaries. Christmas was always a fun time with

Kashi as she wore the bows from the packages around her neck.

They were also with us on that September day in 2001 when the Twin Towers fell. We sat in stunned silence as the second tower was hit on live TV. I think they understood our horror. There were no puppy games that morning. Sutton sat on Ray's lap in the Eames chair and Lexington lay on the floor, putting his paw in Ray's outstretched hand. Gus and Madison snuggled with me. We sat in shock watching the events unfold. We knew people in those towers; we had so many good friends living and working in New York City. We were horrified yet could not take our eyes off of the television. I was so grateful Ray was not on a flight that day. As an United Airlines multi-million-mile flier, every week his travels took him crisscrossing the country, often several planes a day. Grateful, grateful, grateful.

Gus accompanied me to work later that morning and seemed to provide a comfort to the many people we met throughout the day; many who had a story to tell. Customers would sit on the floor with him and tell him about their friend or relative who was in New York that morning or how their flight made an unscheduled stop in Portland and they were stuck in a city where they knew no one. Luggage was lost; people needed clothing to wear until planes were flying again. My shops were busy. Gus sat with many people over the next few days. Some came back in just to see him. Animals understand pain and loss and provide amazing comfort, even to strangers. I am always amazed to watch them at work.

barbara boswell brunner

Milo, Pirates and Reunions

As the official shop dog on Portland's fashionable NW 23rd Ave., Gus knew everyone. He would sit on the front porch of the shop getting sun and head pats from customers passing by. It was a busy street and there were often other dogs, some with their people and some escapees. Lost dogs always managed to find our shop and we always found a way to reunite them with their owners.

There was little itsy bitsy Milo. I left the shop late one evening in the dark. As I walked a block to my car, I kept hearing a soft click, click, click, on the sidewalk behind me. Every time I turned around to see what it was, the sidewalk was empty. I thought I was hearing things. As I approached my car, the clicks were still following me and I turned quickly enough to see the source. There was the tiniest Dachshund I had ever seen, no more than eight or nine inches long. He looked so frightened and cold. I picked him up, tucked him inside my coat and started looking around to see where he might belong. He had a collar but his rabies tag was the only thing attached. I stopped in the sushi restaurant; but no one there knew anything about him. The nail shop was still open and again, no one knew him. There were no other stores open and the streets were void of pedestrians.

At Dove Lewis, they scanned him for an ID chip, but sadly he did not have one. They looked up his rabies registration and said a veterinarian on Portland's east side registered him, almost fifteen miles away. He was barely six months old. How had this little guy managed to get so far from home? I dropped him off at the vet's office for him to await pickup by his owner. She called me the next day to thank me for rescuing Milo. She had no explanation for how he got to my shop. She'd left him in the house when she went to work and when she got home he was gone. No doors were open and nothing had been disturbed. Even if he snuck out the door behind her that morning, how in the world did he get across the river fifteen miles away? I was just glad he found me and they were reunited.

Another little mutt came in on Christmas Eve, wandering right up to Gus. He was clearly lost and it was cold outside.

He just wanted to get warm. He had no collar or tags. We gave him a treat and a bowl of water and when the shop closed for the evening we took him to get scanned for an ID chip. He had none. We couldn't leave this little guy at Dove Lewis; they only took injured dogs. All of the shelters and vet offices were closed for Christmas. Taking him home with us seemed to be the only option. As we drove down the street, the puppy started to whine. Ahead of us was an older man who looked down on his luck and was dressed somewhat like a pirate: a navy and white stripped knit shirt, pea coat, khaki knickers and a skull cap. His long grey stringy hair flowed out of the cap and down his back. All that was missing was the eye patch. Ray had noticed him earlier in the day from the window of my shop and mentioned it was kind of late in the year for Halloween garb.

We passed him, turned the corner and the puppy stopped whining. "That was odd. Ray, let's go back and pass by that man again," I said. As we approached the puppy started to whine again, this time with much more confidence. "I bet that's his owner," Ray exclaimed and pulled over.

I got out of the car and asked the man if he owned a dog. He was sobbing, an inconsolable sob. He said he did have a dog, but he had wandered away the previous day. He was so sad and said he could not bear to spend Christmas without his dog. The copy store had offered to make up some lost dog fliers for him and he was passing them out. I looked at the flier and there was the face of the puppy that had wandered into our shop. I jumped with joy! They were reunited on Christmas Eve. What a Christmas miracle!

New Years Eve that same year brought Fudge, an Burmese Mountain puppy. As I recall he was only a few months old. He spent the night with us, since his owners were not answering their phone. Turns out they were out of town and the puppy sitter was not being very responsible. She did not even know Fudge was missing. The owners were so grateful for our puppy hospitality that we were rewarded with a wonderful bottle of Dom Perignon, Cheers!

Lexington...

By the fall of 2002, Lexington was starting to show his age. He was now almost nine years old with lots of gray on his muzzle. His energy was starting to wane. He could still get around well with the help of his daily Rimadyl tablets, he was just moving a little slower.

Ray and I were traveling more, mostly to Europe. We founded a start-up skin care company, Blue, and were using manufacturing facilities in Nice and Brittany, France. Our house sitter was a wonderful girl who we were introduced to by friends Les and Gerri. She called us on one of our trips to France with a great deal of concern in her voice. She had arrived home from work and found Lexington very ill. He seemed to have an upset stomach. I told her to stop giving his Rimadyl and give him some Pepto Bismol to help coat his stomach. We would be home the following day.

We arrived back in Portland and found Lexington just as the house sitter had said, lethargic and weak. We rushed him to Dr. Ron's office where we received the horrible news. Lexington had liver cancer, which had spread to his pancreas. We left him two weeks earlier and he seemed fine. Cancer took him unfairly fast. We tried multiple medications to make him comfortable over the next week. He was dropping weight like a rock and although he never cried, we sensed he was in pain. He had gone from ninety-five pounds to sixty pounds in three weeks. He was fading rapidly.

Ray was traveling on business again and I could not euthanize Lexington without him. Lexi was HIS dog. For three days I took him to work with me every morning, carrying him up the stairs to my office. I turned the Golf Channel on TV for him. If I had to work in the store I would carry him in and play soft music for him while he lay behind the desk. He was heavily medicated with painkillers and I hope he did not suffer.

When Ray arrived back in Portland, he was shocked at Lexington's continued decline and we did the only humane thing we could do. We called Dr. Ron who came immediately to the house. We did not want Lexi to be in any more pain. We hugged him, held his paws, kissed him on the forehead and told him goodbye. We cried. My heart hurt.

"No Pickles, Please" and the Physic

Lexington was the kindest, most loyal dog and the leader of our brood. He would be missed for a very long time. Gus, Sutton and Madison got to say their goodbyes and later that day we could see a change in Gus. The baton had been passed. He was now taking over as leader of our little pack. He pranced around the girls seemingly to announce his new position. He walked with his head a little higher and a bouncier spring in his step. Madison and Morgan seemed to welcome his authority.

Everyone loved Gus. Brittany Spaniel origins are from the north of France and we often called him the Fancy French Boy. When he got a haircut he would parade around showing off his new "do." He loved to be clean and well groomed and would sit patiently while I clipped and buffed his nails or brushed his teeth. Maybe it was from his years of neglect or maybe he just appreciated the one-on-one mom time. Customers would always make a special effort to come see him on grooming day and admire his new bandana. He soaked up the attention.

He was a ham and always happy to meet new people. His nature was easy going, so what began one afternoon was quite puzzling. A messenger came to the store to drop off proofs for an advertisement we were running in the local paper. Jim was the same messenger we always used and he had been in the store around Gus many times. Suddenly, Gus awoke from his nap, jumped to his feet, charged at Jim and bit him on the calf. It was not a bite that broke the skin, only a bruise, but Jim was frightened and I was mortified. Of course I paid his medical bills and promised to not have Gus on the sales floor any longer. We didn't know it at the time, but Gus was beginning to have seizures. I suspect he had a minor seizure when we thought he was napping and when he came back to awareness, he was startled by Jim and saw him as a threat.

Soon Gus was having seizures every few days. They were awful. He would become very stiff with his legs outstretched. His eyes would roll back in his head. We sought out the advice of a canine neurologist. He did many tests on Gus, MRI, EEG, CAT. Nothing was conclusive. There were no tumors, which was very good. He placed Gus on Phenobarbital to control the seizures. After a week on medication, Gus was a zombie. He stumbled when he walked and slept most of the time; his eyes were glazed. This was not a good quality of life. We conferred with the neurologist and he had no other options to offer. If HE said we should use drugs then that is what we should do.

Ray and I did not accept that answer. Something caused these seizures to start. If it was epilepsy it would have started when he was a puppy. If it had been a trauma we would have seen some damage to his head. We were stumped. I started researching canine seizures on the Internet and spent weeks reading various veterinary web posts. I consulted Dr. Mike, our vet from Tennessee. He connected me with some of his students at Vanderbilt University who were doing studies on canine seizures. They shared their research and references. I dug through the information with a passion. One of their resources discussed food preservative allergies and their relationship to seizures. Hmm. We always fed our dogs the most premium dog food we could find, a well-known veterinarian-recommended brand. I read the ingredients on the bag in the pantry and there it was, the culprit preservative. I was relieved and at the same time furious that such a well-known premium brand of dog food used an ingredient that could cause seizures.

How many other families had gone through this and given their pets unnecessary medications turning their beloved pets into zombies? More research. I had to find a brand that did not contain this particular preservative. At the time there were not as many holistic and natural brands of dog food as there are today. I found ONE brand, a supermarket brand dog food. How ironic, I thought. For all of the years we paid extra for a "premium" brand dog food that made our dog sick and we simply could have been feeding this basic supermarket brand.

We switched his food immediately and within a week the seizures stopped. It was astounding. Now I was on a mission to find the best possible ingredients in dog food. There were just not many options so I started to home cook for them: ground turkey, sweet potatoes, veggie-medleys, oats, eggs and a dash of fresh fruit, usually blueberries and cranberries. I would make up a big batch and keep it in the fridge for a few days. Gus started to lose his extra weight, Madison's and Lexington's coats shone like headlights. It was clear this was the way to go until we could find a dog food brand that met our standards. Gus never had another seizure.

Prior to discovering the preservative issues with dog food, I was frustrated not knowing what was wrong with Gus. I talked about it with everyone I met. A friend told me about a woman who claimed to be able to communicate with animals and relay their thoughts. I had heard of horse whisperers and had no doubt that there could be dog whisperers, but this woman claimed to be able to do it over the phone. Her name was Lydia.

I thought it was crazy, but what harm could it do, I thought? I made all of the arrangements and at our allotted time, I placed the call to Lydia with Gus by my side. I was determined to not give her much information to see what "skills" she really had. I gave her the general information that Gus was a Brittany, adopted by us when he was three and was having seizures. She said she really needed more to go on, but she would work with what little I had given her. She understood my skepticism.

She said Gus had been hit in the head as a youngster by a bright light. She said her interpretation of the images in his mind were that it was lightning or gunfire. Okay, I thought, that is plausible but not so far-fetched for a hunting dog. She said his left ear hurt for a long time, but he did not have headaches from it anymore. She also said she saw an image of him being hit in the head by a ghoulish woman for tearing wallpaper off a wall. Now this was getting weird. Dick and Jane had told us long ago that the original reason Gus was put into his outdoor kennel was for destroying the wallpaper in their bathroom. Hmmm. I was still not a believer, but it was darn coincidental. She also said he had stomachaches and to try switching his food. Truly odd, in light of how things turned out, huh?

Lydia and I talked for a few minutes more and she said our time was up. As we were saying goodbye, she interrupted and asked if there was another dog in the room. I asked why and she said someone needed to talk to her. I told her there were no other dogs in the room, but I had three other dogs in the house. She told me that one of them was trying to get her attention calling "ME, ME, ME." Okay, I thought, I'll bite.... She continued on, saying the images she saw were of a fast-food drive through, a hamburger and a happy dog. Her interpretation was that one of the dogs really liked burgers, but was pleading for her to ask us to not get pickles next time. I hung up with her, dumbfounded. Sutton loved to go to the drive thru at McDonald's and always spit out the pickles.

Always. Every time. No Pickles.

Drama Queens, The Vapors and Cancer

Life was moving at supersonic speed. My business was thriving, Ray was as busy as ever with his consulting work and the dogs were growing into a comfortable routine. Sutton was now four years old. What a beautiful dog she had become, petite but gorgeous. No reminders of her awkward puppy growth. She was very active and played well now with Madison and Gus. We did notice that when Sutton jumped up onto the bed at night she let out a little squeal. Odd, we thought. It continued for a month or so and was getting more pronounced.

I admit it. I am guilty of calling her a drama queen on many occasions. If Sutton had hands, she would have put the back of her hand on her brow and said she had "the vapors." She knew how to work a room, but this time is seemed more real.

Time to get it checked. Dr. Ron did some x-rays and couldn't find much, but since it seemed to be related to jumping it could be something in her spine and he referred us to a specialist in neurology. Dr. Ego with No People Skills, the same man we had taken Gus to for his seizures.

This incredibly abrasive man met with us in his office and suggested we do an MRI and a CAT scan to get more information. Good idea we thought, although expensive, it would be worth knowing what was going on. Dr. EWNPS abruptly took her away and said to go home. He would call with the results. At 6:00 PM we got the news. Sutton had a tumor wrapped around her spine. He did a biopsy and it was benign, but was pinching the spinal cord and causing pain. Eventually it would cripple her. Surgery was our only option. We thought at least we have the self-pronounced best canine neurosurgeon in the Pacific Northwest, Dr. EWNPS.

Sutton's surgery was a success. She was on her feet the same day and walking. We were thrilled and relieved, but now she needed radiation to kill off any remaining tumor. Thirty-five treatments, every day, except for Sunday. I took her to the oncologist every morning and picked her up at lunch. Radiation does not affect dogs the same way it affects people. Her side effects were limited to less energy and a week after the last treatment she seemed back to normal. We wondered if she would also need chemotherapy. Dr. EWNPS said no, he did not recommend it. Between the surgery (which he performed so brilliantly, in his words) and the radiation, Sutton would be fine. We were so thankful and extremely happy. It was so good to have a happy ending to a cancer scare for a change.

Cooper 2003 – 2011

eight weeks old

LOOK at the size of his feet!

The Throw Away Dog

Lexington had now been gone for a few months and his absence was palpable. We also had a gender imbalance and did not want the fighting between the girls to start again. It was time for a new puppy. Seriously, I just can't help myself. I registered with a few rescue organizations in the Portland area, letting them know we were only interested in a young dog and it must be a male. A Rottie or a Dobie would be ideal. Weeks went by and we waited.

I got the phone call in late February 2003. Doberman Rescue had been alerted to a Champion Show Breeder who had a male puppy they were going to put down and asked if I was interested in rescuing it. "Of course," I said without the slightest hesitation. I inquired with what ailment was he afflicted, that they felt it necessary to euthanize. I wanted to know what we would be facing with this puppy. We were happy to adopt a high needs dog, I just needed to know how to prepare. Would we need equipment or special medical supplies? The woman at the rescue sighed heavily and said his affliction was that he was not show quality.

"What does that mean?" I asked. "Well," she hesitated," he has blue eyes and a pink nose; they cannot sell him as a show dog and do not want to be bothered selling him as a pet." My disgust must have been evident in the tone of my voice. She said she agreed. The only special equipment we would need would be love and we had lots of that.

The breeder's farm was two hours away and I knew I had to get there as soon as possible. The rescue woman gave me the phone number and encouraged me to call and arrange a meeting. The breeder told me I could come that evening, so I left my office immediately and headed south to Oregon Wine Country. I arrived after dark and pulled up to the house. Greeting me was a very pleasant woman and her husband, who was not. The woman took me to their kitchen that had been set up as a puppy playroom. There were several puppies rolling and tumbling on the floor.

In the corner was THE puppy. He was hiding behind his momma, Hurricane, a gorgeous black Doberman. Just looking at her I could tell she was a Champion— she was stunning. The puppy was huge, so much bigger than the other puppies. First born often are, but he was at least twice the other's size. I sat on the floor and all of the puppies crawled up on my lap for kisses, except for the red one. He sat in the corner and stared at me. The breeder said he was very shy. She sat down and he ran to her and snuggled. I knew she was not the one who wanted to euthanize this puppy; she had an obvious bond with him. She brought him over to me and he willingly crawled up on my lap, still staring at me with great curiosity. Who was this strange woman, I am sure he thought. She has the same color hair and eyes as I do!

The puppy wore a beautiful shade of red fur, so thin his pinkish skin glimmered through. His bright blue eyes were shining and his bulbous pink nose was sniffing my scent. His feet and teeth were huge. I've seen a lot of puppies through the years, but never one so big for his age. He was sizing me up and I gave him points for being smart and intuitive.

We played for a while with a tiny stuffed giraffe, his favorite toy. I threw it and he lopped to it with a clumsy puppy gait, grabbed it, ran back and handed it to me. I had to take this guy home; I knew he was special. Eventually I asked what paperwork we needed to complete the transaction. She said "nothing." It was clear they wanted to erase this puppy from existence. The husband gave me a binder with copies of the pedigree, photos of the dame and sire and the puppy's baby photos. He asked that we not register him with the AKC as it would hurt their show dog's lineage. What a jerk.

It was very cold that night and felt like snow. I had a blanket with me to keep the puppy warm. I wrapped him up and placed him on the front passenger seat, turning on the seat heater. I did not see her do it, but the woman quietly tucked the little stuffed giraffe into the blanket cave. I did not see it until I got him home. She was going to miss this little guy. I called Ray and told him what I had done and you could hear the enthusiasm in his voice. He couldn't wait to meet our new addition.

Bringing him home and introducing him to the other dogs was concerning; how would they react, how would Gus adjust, being the new pack leader. I brought in the little bundle with trepidation and placed him on the living room floor. Gus took his turn first, investigating all of the important parts and walked away somewhat disinterested. I was actually surprised Gus didn't pee on him. He did that to everything he wanted to own. Madison licked him up and down from top to bottom. The little guy seemed to look to her as his new momma. Sutton took one look at him and said, "Let's PLAY!!" She bowed on the floor in puppy play mode and romped with him all over the kitchen. They chased each other, slid around corners and had a grand time. He was a wonderful addition to our family, I decided, and went to bed that night with him sleeping soundly in a crate beside the bed. He was our first dog that LOVED the crate immediately. It was his man cave and a place he could protect his stuffed toys from Madison and her jaws of death. He kept his little giraffe safe and I still have it today.

Naming him was a challenge. We had to watch him for almost a week until we finally decided on the perfect name. I was in love with the new Mini Cooper. They were just starting to import them to the U.S. and I had ordered one of the first ones. The car I ordered was chili red with a black convertible top. An email arrived informing me my car was out of production and on the boat to the U.S. "Your Cooper has been born," the email said and it hit me. Cooper was the perfect name for our new guy. My car was red and he was red. My car was peppy and cute and he certainly fit that description, too.   Cooper took to his new name instantly and would cock his head when we called his name. I think he liked it.

Dr. Ron thought Cooper was hilarious. He was skittish with anyone new but Dr. Ron would get down on the floor to greet him on his own level.   They connected. That seemed to work well and Cooper was never scared of going to the vet.   Dr. Ron also thought Cooper was huge for his age. At seven weeks old he already weighed twenty-one pounds.   He suspected Cooper was going to be a very big boy.

Woo,Woo,Woo

On the day Cooper was to be neutered, we dropped him off in the morning and left him in the hands of the very competent staff. As they started to run his IV line, the tech was not happy with the flow and decided to move the line to a better vein. He couldn't get the blood to clot in the first insertion point. It just continued to bleed. I imagine there was plenty of scurrying around trying to determine what was wrong. His second IV line was in, and after some quick thinking by Dr. Ron, Cooper was transfused with platelets. They got the bleeding stopped.

Cooper had Von Willebrand's Deficiency, a lack of clotting factor in the blood similar to hemophilia in humans. It is an inherited genetic defect all breeding Dobermans should be tested for. Thirty-five percent of all Dobermans have the gene mutation and seventy percent are asymptomatic carriers. Responsible Doberman breeders are now working very hard, through genetic testing, to eliminate this gene mutation from the breed. What this meant for Cooper was that he would have to be infused with clotting factor the day before any surgery and Dr. Ron would always have to keep it on hand for emergencies. What it meant for Cooper's breeder was that they had to retire their two beautiful champions and not allow any more puppies to be born from them. It's funny how things work out sometimes.

VWD made life with Cooper challenging. We had to try to keep him calm, he needed to avoid situations where he could fall and get hurt. He bruised easily and was often seen sporting a big black eye from playing too hard. Every time we moved we had to tell the new neighbors about his clotting problem so that they could inform us quickly if they ever saw him get injured. Everyone looked out for Cooper.

Training him would be critically important and even though we trusted Academy of Canine Behavior with all of our other dogs, we did not want them to be responsible for him with his VWD. We first tried puppy classes to get him accustomed to other dogs. He was terrified of a Dachshund that barked at him. He returned the bark making a sound that reminded us of Curly from the Three Stooges. Woo, woo, woo... just like Curly!

It was so hard not to laugh at him. Woo Woo Boy found many uses for that bark through the years, mostly to let us know there was something intruding into his personal air space. Following puppy classes were private trainers. He learned his commands quickly and walked well on a leash. We walked through downtown Portland every day exposing him to all kinds of new sights and sounds. He came when called, sat on command and did a pretty darned good stay. Our most useful command through the years though, was FREEZE! It saved him many, many times. A glass broken on the floor, an electric car on the street that couldn't be heard, or a door left mistakenly open. Freeze was a multi-functional command to get him to stop immediately. He was a very good puppy and tried so hard to please us.

I took a wire crate into work so I could spend more time with Cooper and help his training progress. Every time Ray would call to check in and ask what Cooper was doing the answer was always the same. "Sleeping."

8:00 AM—sleeping

12:00 PM—sleeping

4:00 PM—sleeping

I swear to this day, you could watch him grow while he slept. If he wasn't sleeping, he was playing with his stuffed purple hippo, his new best friend. We would play a few rounds of chase during the day, but Cooper usually started yawning and went back to sleep. He had a lot of growing to do.

At the shop, his crate door was never shut and customers would come in and play with him. We wanted to expose him to as many new things as we could in his first few months to get him well socialized. He was still very cautious around anyone new; it took him awhile to warm up. He had to analyze the situation first and decide if there was any danger. Woo, woo, woo was frequently heard up and down the street. Once he got to know you, though, you were his friend for life.

Sophie was his favorite visitor. She was the eight-year-old granddaughter of a customer who would come every week to visit and play with him and his purple hippo. She had no fear of such a big dog and he adored her. Sophie and her family moved away and their visits stopped. I never knew how much her visits registered with Cooper until years later when she came to visit her grandparents. She was now a teenager and twice as tall as she had been when she knew Cooper. He was a lot bigger too, having grown from twenty-one pounds to a hundred-ten pounds. She came in to see Cooper and I told her he was now too big to have in the shop every day, but I would bring him the following day so she could see him. She was waiting for us as we arrived and shouted, "Cooper!" His little stub of a tail started wagging; he bolted toward her, put his paws on her shoulders and gave her a big sloppy kiss. He remembered her! They played for hours.

Cooper was quirky and without a doubt the smartest of all of our dogs. He was also a con artist and a food thief. He would counter surf when no one was looking and steal whatever he could. He has been known to steal steaks off the grill, entire blocks of cheese from the kitchen counter, but his favorite was butter. He would steal that right out from under our noses, with no hesitation. He could swallow an entire stick of butter in two seconds flat and even knew how to unwrap it. He stuck his head in our bullet trashcan trying to retrieve some random food tidbit and I thought I would pass out from laughter as he tried to get his head uncaught from the swinging lid.

He was a pie thief. Ray bought a

cherry pie for dinner, placed it on the kitchen counter and walked out of the room for a moment. When he returned, there was Cooper with the full pie and pan in his mouth looking like a Maasai warrior prince. One year he ate half of the Thanksgiving turkey. He would steal apples from the fruit bowl and like a magpie he would steal anything shiny. Car keys, cell phones and jewelry all fell victim to Cooper. Some items he would hide in his bed. High value items would get buried in the yard. I am still missing a silver Razor phone from 2006...

He had unusual eating habits. Cooper would grab a mouthful of kibble and carry it to any table of his liking, a coffee table, the dining room table or the seat of an expensive leather chair where he would proceed to eat it one kibble at a time. He did this at every meal, every day, his entire life. If there were no table available he would take the food to his bed, lay each kibble out in a line on the floor and eat. Cooper's slobber mixed with kibble dust made an amazing adhesive, better than super glue. We have a wooden bench we had to sand to remove his slobber. He chewed water instead of lapping it—schlomp, schlomp, schlomp— throwing water everywhere around the room.

Cooper eventually outgrew his crate, began sleeping in our bed and discovered COVERS! At night he would stand by the pillows and wait for the blanket to be lifted so he could crawl under to the foot of the bed and get cozy. He would often stand straight up in the middle of the night and imitate a ghost on Halloween, scaring the heck out of us. If he got too hot he would sneak up to the pillows, select one to rest his head on, while still covered with blankets. Ray and I would wake and roll over to say good morning, only to be met with Cooper's big body in between us, snoring on a pillow.

Cooper lining up his kibble

Cooper in the snow in Portland

It's SNOWING... Pluuuzzzeeee, May I Go Outside?

Cooper grew to enormity. His head could rest easily on the dining table and at a slight tilt on the kitchen counter. His feet were the size of my hands. He was a big, strong boy looking more like a Great Dane than a Doberman. His beautiful blue puppy eyes turned hazel as he grew older. He had enormous teeth; even Dr. Ron said they were "freakishly large teeth;" his quote, not mine. I thought they were beautiful. They were optic white and looked like he used bleaching strips when no one was looking. His teeth were the first thing strangers would comment on. They almost glowed in the dark. As he aged, he became a butt nipper. It was his way of showing affection, although it startled many folks. He only did it to people he liked and would usually catch them off guard as they were walking away. It may have been his way of saying, "stay here with me, please." Big Doberman, BIG teeth and butts were at exactly the right height.

Even with his food thievery, Cooper was as skinny as a rail. What I would pay for that metabolism. No matter how much he ate, he never gained weight. Each new vet we would see over the years always said he needed to gain a few pounds.

He loved to give "nose kisses" putting his feet on my shoulders and lightly touching just the tip of my nose with his. If he needed anything during the night he would nudge me gently with his nose. If I did not wake up in the time frame he thought suitable, one nudge became two or three. He kept at it until I was fully awake and ready to attend to his needs. Often it was just to lift the covers so he could get back into bed.

Cooper was quirky. If he were human he would have worn an ascot, a smoking jacket and used a cigarette holder. Even with his enormous size, he had elegance about him. He was as graceful as a racehorse and as strong as an elephant.

Cooper was also childlike. He loved the snow. He seemed to have a sixth sense and would know when a snowstorm was coming. He would wait by the window and the minute the first flakes started to fall announce the snow's arrival by dancing with joy. It did not matter what hour of the day or night it was, he wanted to go outside and catch snowflakes. He would catch them on his tongue and run in delight as they melted. On many occasions I would get a nose nudge in the middle of the night to announce a storm had arrived. If that did not get me to arise, my covers would soon disappear, being carried off the bed in Cooper's mouth. He was persistent. He loved the snow. After waking me up he would have a look on his face like a five-year-old seeing their first snow. His eyes would be huge and I can imagine him saying, "Mom, mom,mom...it's SNOWING...pluuuzzzeeee, may I go outside."

Cooper and Sutton would chase each other, chest butting for hours and flopping in the snowdrifts. I do think he would have preferred a snowsuit, though, perhaps one from Hermes, to fulfill his need to be hip and fashionable. He did not like being cold.

barbara boswell brunner

Deck Diving

Cooper and Sutton played hard. They loved to chase each other in a fast game of tag. Up and down the hill, around the koi ponds and back up the deck stairs. They had a ball. The summer of 2003 was stifling. We had several days with temperatures over one-hundred degrees and weeks over ninety. It was not normal for Portland and we did not have air conditioning. The dogs were very hot so we bought them a kiddie splash pool for the deck. Cooper devised a game of chase involving diving from the hot tub deck down to the splash pool, sliding across and out of the pool and around their usual racecourse. They had a ton of fun with that pool. He and Sutton were thick as thieves and they never stopped running that summer.

By fall, Sutton was again yipping when she jumped onto the bed. Denial was our method of coping, until we finally succumbed to the reality that her pain had returned. We made an appointment with Dr. Ego With No People Skills one more time. He thought her pain was most likely caused by scar tissue that had formed around the original surgery, but when we received the results of her MRI, we were devastated. The tumor was back and it was growing with a vengeance. It was not only wrapped around her spinal cord, it was also running through her vertebrae.

We were angry with ourselves for not listening to the oncologist twelve months earlier, who had suggested chemotherapy. Dr. EWNPS performed another surgery and this time it did not go well. Sutton did not recover. She was paralyzed. Dr. EWNPS said he had done all for her that he could and suggested I make her comfortable at home until Ray returned later in the week.

They carried her to my car on a stretcher with a friend meeting me at home to carry her inside. Sutton lay on her bed for three days, unable to move anything but her head and neck. Cooper snuggled with her on the bed keeping her company. He brought her favorite toys. Another friend came by three times a day to help me flip her, clean her and feed her. Sutton was frightened and did not understand why she couldn't move. It was ghastly, although having her final days at home with her family was a small consolation. All of the dogs had a chance to spend time with her. They seemed to understand the gravity of her situation and were so gentle. Cooper cuddled with her at night and Gus guarded her during the day. Ray arrived home Thursday evening, sleeping on the floor with her all night. Dr. Ron arrived the next morning, with his supplies in hand.

Our goodbyes were said. Madison, Cooper and Gus sniffed the body as Dr. Ron and Ray carried Sutton to the van. They understood. Although we were sad, it was not the crushing loss we felt in the past. The extra year we got to spend with her was a special gift.

Sutton was at peace.

Cooper with Morgan at six weeks old

Pick Me...Pick Me

Cooper's face was always very expressive and his mourning for Sutton was obvious. His furrowed brow and heartbreaking eyes let us know to what extent he missed her. His playmate was gone and Madison was no substitute. Stealing his stuffed animals and shredding them was her version of playing. Cooper took meticulous care of his stuffed toys. He had his purple Hippo for more than a year before Madison killed it. We could never find another to replace it. His Donkey had a noisemaker that honked. Every time Madison killed a Donkey we had to rush to the store for a replacement. Thank goodness they were readily available. Our house was filled with Donkeys in various stages of demise, but Cooper always had to have one with the functioning honker, knowing exactly where to press the nose to make him talk. He LOVED his collection of stuffed animals and he loved to make them talk. We bought him a huge white elephant we called Ellie. She was as big as Cooper. When he first saw Ellie his eyes lit up with excitement. He carried her around the house and cuddled with her at night. He had to prance like a Lipizzaner to keep Ellie from tripping him as he carried her from his bed to the sofa to the patio.

One afternoon a customer told me about a local Rottweiler breeder who had a litter of eight puppies. There were deposits on most, but a couple of them were still available. Okay, okay. I am really NOT a hoarder, really...I just cannot resist puppy breath. Maybe a new puppy would make Cooper happy. He was just a year old and needed a friend his own size he could play hard with. A Rottie seemed like a good choice. Our decision to go to a breeder this time was slightly influenced by the high medical costs we had from all the dogs we had rescued. We could really appreciate a dog from good lineage without medical issues, for a change, and we wanted a big healthy dog to be Cooper's playmate. We made an appointment for the weekend, when Ray would be home. He really missed Lexington and Sutton and was eager to find another Rottie.

When we arrived at the farm, all of the dogs came running to meet us. They had just been moved from the house to the barn and were getting the run of the place. They seemed very well-adjusted and the momma and papa were beautiful. They were German Rottweiler—very stocky and muscular with the most adorable short snouts. They looked like black bear cubs. All of them were extremely friendly and excited to see us. The owner took the parents back to the barn and left us alone with the puppies in the corral. How cute! They were running and tumbling in the grass, flopping around and jumping on each other. We were not yet sure which puppies were spoken for and did not want to fall in love with any particular one. We played with them all, but one kept sitting on Ray's foot. He would move toward another puppy and it would follow and sit on his foot again. It had either claimed Ray or was saying, "pick me, pick me." When the owner came back to the corral she laughed at the tubby lump of fur attached to Ray's foot. As it turned out, it was the only female still available. She was a beauty, only six weeks old but well-adjusted and since we were experienced dog owners the breeder let her go home with us that day. We named her Morgan.

We introduced her to the family on our deck in Portland, each individually since she was so young. We didn't want to overwhelm her. Gus was first. He sniffed her butt in the usual doggie fashion, nudged her onto her back and licked her.

She had passed the Gus test. Madison was next. She was not too interested, probably thinking, geeze, I just got rid of my archenemy and now they bring home a clone?? She trotted off, clearly not happy.

Cooper was last. He was not good with new anything, let alone a new puppy. We knew he would be the tough judge. We sat them on the deck together to take a photo. Cooper is immortalized on film looking at her with a terrified look on his face. I picture a bubble over his head that says "oh, my god, oh my god, it's going to kill me..." This giant-sized animal was not so sure about the little 14-ounce squirt that nipped at his toes. And it barked and everything! Morgan got down on her belly and slid up to him, rolled over on her back and lay still. She seemed to know he was afraid. She gave him a chance to warm up and then she was off...across the deck and down the hill with Cooper in fast pursuit. A toy that squeaked AND played back, Cooper thought! Whoo hoo!

Our friends Dane and Ellen met Morgan the week we brought her home. Ellen said Morgan reminded her of her mother's old baseball glove, circa 1930: soft, hand-sized, and perfectly floppy. Who knew that in later years Morgan would begin to look more like a manatee than a dog?

Morgan adjusted quickly to her new family. Cooper was still using his crate and we didn't have room for another. We chose to house Morgan in our master bathroom with a gate across the door. It was certainly big enough and had granite floors, so she could not do any damage. We were in the planning stages of a remodel and there was nothing in there she could destroy that mattered. She could still see us but would not be free to roam the house at night and get into trouble. She was not used to sleeping alone. When we got up in the morning, there she was hiding under the toilet tank, crunched up against the wall; her bed not touched. It's the spot she chose as hers for the next few months until she got too big to fit.

Morgan never chewed anything growing up. Not a shoe, a cabinet door nor a sofa. She was perfectly behaved. She learned her commands so quickly that we did not feel any need to send her to Academy for training. Her behavior was perfect and she was smart. Cooper kept her company and they played from dusk to dawn. He shared his toys, which she never destroyed, and cared for her as lovingly as he did his stuffed animals. He was her protector. Madison tried to pick fights with Morgan when she was a baby, with

Morgan never responding. As Morgan grew to manatee size, Madison wisely decided to make peace with her.

I took Morgan to work with me for the first few months and her favorite spot to hang out was under a display cabinet that tucked against the wall by my office. She could watch the front door of the shop and be ready for anyone who wanted to pat her head. She loved people and most days we let her run free in the shop, greeting customers. As she grew, more and more people would ask, "She is so beautiful and friendly, what breed is she?" Of course this was after they had been on the floor playing with her and letting their two-year-olds sit on her. When we replied "Rottweiler," they would gasp, grab their children and rush off.

Rottweiler are so misunderstood. They are very smart, friendly and would much rather watch the insides of their eyelids from a sofa than do much else. I started tethering her to the bookshelves in my office with a twenty-five foot cable so customers could feel more secure. Her last day in the shop was the day she pulled those bookshelves out onto the sales floor. She was getting incredibly strong.

Morgan had a chance to meet a sibling when she was about six months old. A customer was shopping and noticed her in my office and of course had to play with her. She and her husband also had a Rottie about the same age. As we talked we realized we had puppies from the same litter. The following day she brought Bear back to see Morgan. We were unsure if they would remember one another, but they seemed to recognize each other instantly. They rolled around like they did in the corral the day we met them except now they each weighed fifty pounds. A little puppy-tumbling turned into wrestling. They chased each other, knocking over a few displays but I didn't care. It was just so fun to watch. When they were told to stop, each came over and lay at our feet although a little mouth wrestling was still going on. It was a good reunion.

Morgan 2004 –

five years old

The Six Million Dollar Dog?

Like most Rottweiler, Morgan was stoic and introspective. She never complained when in pain and it took us a while to figure out she was having trouble with her front legs. She was limping, but it was never on the same side. Sometimes left, sometimes right. It was less of a limp and more of an odd gait. It was puzzling. Dr. Ron looked at her and referred us to an orthopedic vet. The bones in her front legs had grown at two different speeds, leaving one bone in each leg longer than it should be. This resulted in dislocated shoulders. Ouch!

Surgery was the only answer and we could only do one leg at a time. The longer bone had to be whittled down to the same length as the shorter bone so the shoulder could work properly. Pins needed to be inserted to insure the bones stayed in place over the six-month healing process. We did the left leg first and in six months, just as she was getting around again we did the right leg. The poor girl was confined for almost a full year. She never complained or cried and accepted her situation. We set up our family room as a dog room so she wouldn't be so confined as in a cage. She got us totally to herself at night when we watched TV, which made her feel special.

Just as she was being allowed to leave her dog room and start playing with Cooper again, she ran around the corner from the kitchen to the living room, slid on the hardwood floor and blew her left ACL. Morgan was back to the confines of the dog room for another twelve weeks. We talked to the breeder and to others who bought puppies from the same litter. Not a single one had this problem, in fact one had just won best of breed in a regional dog show and another was working on agility trials. The vet could not explain it, it was just one of those one in a million happenings. Her bones were very delicate for such a large animal and this could have been a contributing factor. He said it was only a matter of time before she blew her right ACL.

I think somewhere in Doggie Heaven there is a Most Wanted poster with Ray's and my photo posted prominently. The caption would read, "If you are sick, injured or in need of very expensive medical care, FIND THESE HUMANS!"

If you are sick, injured or in need of expensive medical care: FIND THESE HUMANS!

Morgan was finally healed and she, Madison and Cooper played constantly. Their games of chase up and down our hill were like an Olympic sport. It would wear them out, keep them in good physical shape and give Gus a break so he could rest.

Gus was once again the shop dog. My office had moved to one of my new shops and he was content to lie in the doorway and watch the customers come and go. His seizure issues were long behind us and I had no concern that he would misbehave. Lake Oswego was a very dog-friendly community and customers would bring their dogs into the store to meet Gus. He was livin' large. Every afternoon we would go for a walk and get some exercise. Occasionally he would decide to go to the lake without benefit of a leash or me, causing a throng of people to follow him. Customers would point and say, "He went that way" or they would stick their head in our door and say, "Gus is duck hunting again." Everyone in this small community knew Gus. He and I had to have a talk about the ducks. They were not there for him to chase. They would quack at him and although he never hurt any, in the spring when there were babies he had to stay inside.

Arthritis was setting in and old age was creeping closer. Gus's pace slowed on our walks, with him occasionally tripping and hitting his chin on the ground. He always got up, dusted himself off, and continued proudly on his trek with his head held high. He tripped on one afternoon walk breaking two of his lower front teeth. It was time for Gus to slow down. In his head he was still a young whippersnapper; his body would just not cooperate. Gus was very dignified and getting old was not something he relished. He could no longer run fast and jump high, but we thought for thirteen he was doing great. He loved to be with me and was very sad when he had to stay home. I tried to take him to work with me as much as I could during those days. The thought of him dying alone at home was more than I could bear.

Madison, Cooper and Morgan held down the fort at home. They were in a good routine. They had lots of exercise and plenty of time to watch the inside of their eyelids. They had important dreams to dream.

Butter Boy

Butter Boy

Cooper's food thievery escalated. Our pantry/laundry room was the path that the dogs had to pass through to get to their dog door. The cabinets were floor to ceiling, full of food stuffs—non-perishables, canned goods and snacks. We were well prepared for any emergency the Pacific Northwest could throw at us; snowstorms, volcanoes or earthquakes. We were well supplied.

Nothing was safe from Cooper. I would come home from work and find him with several cans of soup in his bed, or a roll of paper towels. He had not tried to open and eat it, he just wanted to possess it. Ray and I started finding the refrigerator door open and both thought the other had just left it open accidentally until one day we both returned home from a shopping trip and found Cooper on the floor happily chomping on sticks of butter he had pulled off the shelf, thus earning the name "Butter Boy."

If Cooper had thumbs, I think he would have been a chef. He would watch Ray intently as he prepared dinner every night. He was, of course, looking for a handout or opportunities to steal butter but I also think he enjoyed watching the process of cooking. He loved to be the taste tester and was quite honest about his likes and dislikes. I made homemade ice cream and experimented with many unusual flavors. Cooper was always there watching and waiting. Once the ingredients had been mixed, he would get a taste. If he liked it his tail would wag. If it was not good, he sat down, cocked his head with a look on his face that said "REALLY? You're going to serve THAT tonight?"

We Didn't Do It, We Didn't Do It

My business had me frequently in New York and with Ray's legendary travel schedule we needed a reliable house sitter. One who could look after four dogs was a challenge. We went through a few before we found a keeper. One of the sitters had a bit of a wild streak and liked to go clubbing at night. One evening she left the dogs alone too long and they got bored. I received a call at my hotel from our alarm company and the police. Our glass break alarm had been tripped and when the police arrived, there were four sad little faces claiming no responsibility for the big chair that had been knocked through the front window. Another sitter had a great party that included stair dancing with red wine. We had wine splattered from the top of the stairs to the bottom. She clearly loved the dogs and was sad when we no longer called her, but we needed someone with a quiet social life. The dogs were like our children and we could not accept a sitter who did not give them his or her undivided attention.

Finally we found Arianna. Oh, what a gem she was. Attentive, responsible and she loved the dogs. She was recommended by an employee of mine and came with great references. The dogs all seemed to really like her and after she had been sitting for us for more than a year we found out how much.

Arianna's day job was being the public spokesperson for the local power company. I turned on the TV before going to bed and was watching a breaking news story about a huge fire on the east side of Portland. The power grid for that area was shut down due to the intensity of the fire and Arianna was being interviewed about the outage. As she spoke on TV, Cooper and Morgan sat intently listening to her when Cooper walked up and nose-kissed the TV. How sweet! Arianna sat for the dogs until the day we left Portland. We could always depend on her in a pinch and she cared for the kids as though they were her own. She treated our home with respect and we never had any doubt about the care and attention the dogs were receiving from her.

The Friendly Skies...
Extraordinarily Friendly

We bought our retirement home in 2004. We thought that retirement was far off in the future but we wanted a home on Florida's waterfront and knew prices would only be going up. We did a lot of research and found a home in Punta Gorda, a sweet tiny town on Florida's Gulf Coast. The house was modern with high ceilings and waterfront. It was exactly what we were looking for.

Then Hurricane Charley hit; a Category 4 storm with a hundred forty mile-per-hour winds. The eye of the hurricane passed directly over our home. We spent six months putting the house back into livable condition and two years going back and forth from Portland to work with our contractor on the remodel. We would visit every two months and spend two weeks. It was a long time to be away from all of the dogs. We thought it would be nice to take one with us and Madison was the logical choice. She loved to ride in the car and we thought she would do well on the plane. Gus was too old to fly and Cooper and Morgan were too big to fly commercial. We still had our airline crate from our travels with Kashi and Madison fit it perfectly.

Our first trip to Florida was just Mom and Madison. We were connecting through Chicago's O'Hare International Airport. I was very nervous. I had not flown with a dog since the mid 1980's. Back in the old days we could accompany the crate until it was loaded onto the plane. After 9/11 that was no longer possible. I sat by the window at the gate in O'Hare, watching first for her crate to unload from my Portland plane and then racing to the connecting gate, watching and waiting for her to be loaded onto the connecting flight. I double- and triple-checked with the gate attendant. He was a very sweet man and said he was also a flight attendant on the connecting flight.

"We won't leave without her," he assured with a sweet southern twang.

He offered to go down to the tarmac to check on her, giving her a drink of water and a bone. He reported back that she was barking but seemed fine. Eventually they loaded her crate onto the plane and I watched her disappear up the conveyor. I gathered my things together and boarded the plane. As I walked down the jet way I heard barking, LOTS of barking. I said out loud to no one in particular, "This is NOT good." With a big smile, the flight attendant says, "At least we know she's on board." I love an optimist...

Madison vocalized during the entire trip from Chicago to Fort Myers and on the small Embraer Air plane we could hear every bark. Passengers were concerned and called the flight attendant. Was the dog below in distress? Should we make an emergency landing to attend to the dog? It was nice to hear people express concern and not complaints. The flight attendant appreciated it as well and started serving everyone free wine. Several passengers followed me to baggage claim just to make sure she was really okay. On our flight back to Portland we had the good fortune of getting the same flight attendant. I imagine he put in for a transfer that afternoon.

The Transportation and Safety Administration (the TSA) "Experience" was always interesting with Madison. No one at the TSA really knew what the rules were. Some officers wanted to examine her in the crate; others wanted her out of the crate. One was actually going to put her on the belt and x-ray her like a suitcase. It was always entertaining and Madison did a great job of staying calm. We got the skinny from United Airlines on the rules and knew what needed to be done, even if the TSA did not. The airline was required to give you a perforated tag for the crate, which was the crate's boarding pass. It had a detachable section that was to be handed back to the passenger once the animal was loaded onto the plane. If that section was not handed to the passenger connected with the animal, the plane could not take off.

On a returning flight after our fourth trip taking Madison, we had our first, and ultimately last, big problem. We were connecting through Dulles International Airport in Washington, DC. It was wintertime. Rain was falling, cold and hard. We glimpsed Madison's crate on the tarmac but had not yet been handed her tag. The flight was late for take-off and there seemed to be some disagreement brewing among the flight attendants as they started to close the door.

Ray jumped up and said, "WAIT, I don't have the ticket stub for my dog yet."

The flight attendant called the Captain, who said he knew the dog was on the plane. He was positive and we should not worry. Ray was told to sit down, as the plane was ready to taxi to the runway. Ray insisted, "I want the tag and I have the right to hold up the plane until I get it."

There was muffled conversation between the head flight attendant and the cockpit. Eventually a baggage handler boarded the plane. He asked Ray to come with him to the tarmac. Madison's crate was not on board, as Ray had feared. The crate was exactly where we had seen it an hour before. The baggage handler explained that he was worried that Madison was injured. She was holding up her front paw and standing on only three legs. If she was injured they were not permitted to load her. Taking the Captain's word, we would have taken off and Madison would have been left sitting on the tarmac, alone in Washington DC. Ray was furious. He checked her thoroughly and determined that she was fine. She was holding up her paw because she was freezing. She had been sitting outside for more than an hour in mid-30 degree temperatures. That was the last trip for Madison. Shipping her was too risky when she had to travel as cargo. If only we had a smaller dog that could fit under the seat in the cabin, we thought wistfully.

Cooper 2003 - 2011

five years old

Super Cooper, Super Hero

In early 2007, Cooper started jumping up onto my chest and bouncing off, as though to say "tag, you're it." It was odd and something he had never done before. I thought he just wanted nose kisses and patted him on the head. Every day after work, he ran to greet me and did the same thing again; jumped onto my chest in the same spot and bounced off. This was not a fun game of tag! His jumping continued until I had a bruise the size of a silver dollar. My goodness, his aim was accurate-—he kept hitting the same darn spot. I explained to him that was not a proper greeting, but since his language skills were lacking, he probably just heard "lalalalalala." I tried to get him to stop. It was not like him to disobey a command but he was relentless.

After a few weeks of this, I noticed a small lump had formed under the bruised area and had my doctor check it out. She said it was nothing to worry about. It was probably just a cyst that formed from the impact of Cooper's jump and suggested we schedule an outpatient procedure to remove it just to eliminate any concern if it showed up on a future mammogram.

On the day of surgery, Cooper jumped again, this time with Ray watching. He corrected Cooper and made him sit. Cooper seemed frustrated.

We weren't worried about the surgery, being told it was a fairly routine operation. The surgeon came into the prep area, introduced himself and explained what he would be doing. He would make just a small incision and pop out the cyst, quick and easy. I would be in recovery in less than fifteen minutes. I was whisked off to the operating room and when I got the first dose of anesthesia I was asleep instantly. "OUCH" I heard myself mumbling. "That hurt." I heard a rustle in the room and the doctor saying, "Oh my god, what is that?" and I drifted off again into a haze of more anesthesia.

Two hours later I was waking up in the recovery room. The surgeon came to tell me what he had found. Ray already knew. Under the cyst that Cooper had created from his jumping was a three centimeter tumor far back against my chest wall. It could not be felt and did not show up in the mammogram I had just six months earlier. I had breast cancer, Stage 3. It was invasive; it was a high-grade tumor—it was bad.

Ray and I were in shock. We wanted to know more. How long had the tumor been there? Had it spread? We needed information. We went home and I was greeted by Cooper who gently nudged me. He never jumped up on me again. Ever. He must have sensed or smelled the cancer and jumping was the only way he could express his warning. Had the cancer gone undetected much longer, I could have been Stage 4, incurable cancer. Cooper saved my life.

The next year was a whirlwind of doctors, more surgery, chemotherapy and radiation. It was a blur. I had to sleep in a "clean room" at night. No dogs allowed. I was too susceptible to infection. Ray set up a wonderful space for me in the guestroom right across the hall from the master bedroom. Gus lay across my doorway every night guarding my room. Cooper still slept in the master bedroom, but he watched my doorway from his bed. When Ray was out of town, Morgan slept leaning against the front door. I had good guardians.

Ray was in a regular travel routine that year. He came with me to chemotherapy on Monday and left for his office in San Francisco on Tuesday. The side effects from chemo took several days to kick in, so I was fine being alone on Tuesday and Wednesday but was feeling less than chipper by Thursday and so glad that was the night he came home every week. On the days Ray was out of town the dogs never let me out of their sight. They appeared to take turns watching over me and followed me everywhere I went. They were my guardians and my caretakers.

Are You Insane??

On chemo day, Ray and I got into a routine of going very early in the morning for my infusion and to a movie in the afternoon. This was a great way for us to be entertained and keep both of our minds off cancer without taxing me too much. If I was tired from chemo, I could sleep. The theater we frequented was attached to a shopping mall and if the movie did not start for a bit, we would take a walk around the mall and look in the stores. I loved to stop in the pet shop to look at the puppies. (Have I mentioned that I have a serious addiction?) It was a very busy, well run, clean shop and puppies never stayed there very long. However, there was one little terrier that we saw week after week. She was such a cutie; all white with one single black spot on her head and a black stripe and polka dot on one ear. She had little white whiskers forming that looked like snowflakes.

It was October 2007 and I had a monumental birthday approaching. My chemo had been going well and the current cocktail of drugs did not make me feel ill. I had my energy coming back. This was going to be a good birthday. Ray was stumped for a gift. A party was not anything I was interested in. I had every possible piece of jewelry I could want. He was struggling for an idea and finally asked what I would like. Without hesitation and not missing a beat I said the little white dog from the pet shop.

Oh my god. Is she insane?

Five dogs?

Has my wife lost her mind?

"No" isn't something you can say to a cancer patient, right? As we entered the shop, we realized she was not in her usual cage. Oh no, I thought, she's finally been adopted. I suspect "thank goodness" ran through Ray's head, although he vehemently denies it. We talked to the manager and he said she was still there but she was in isolation. She had developed a cough and they wanted to keep her away from the other puppies while she was being treated. He brought her to us in the play area and, yes, she did have a cough. A very bad cough. She had pneumonia. Now, if you remember that poster of us in Doggie Heaven, you know the ending to this tale. She left with us, cuddled tightly in my arms, directly to Dr. Ron's office. He checked her out, read the list of vaccinations she had already received and made notes for her next visit. He sent us home with antibiotics and said she would be fine in a few days. He wondered how she would get along with the big dogs and warned us to introduce her slowly so we did not frighten her. She was very tiny.

A year or so later we discovered her puppy illnesses, including her pneumonia were all a result of allergies. They would result in dozens of trips to several specialists, custom-made vaccines she would need to have injected every week for the rest of her life and many medicines a day to keep her from having allergy attacks. Izzy is allergic to pollen of every kind—grass and floral, insects, dust mites, turkey, beef, pork, chicken, all grains, and all grasses. She had skin allergies, food allergies and inhaled allergies. The Most Wanted Poster was apparently still hanging prominently at the Doggie Distribution Center...

We could not decide on a name. With Morgan and Cooper we were on a car name kick and there were just no car names that seemed to fit her. We could have called her Bug, but that was the nickname of one of our dearest friends. I didn't think she would appreciate us naming our puppy after her. We thought and thought and after a week we decided on Isabella. It seemed to suit her well and was quickly shortened to Izzy, which was perfect for her busy nature. Busy Izzy. Through the years she would also be referred to as Baby Girl, Peanut, Sweet Pea and Cujo.

Izzy was just seven tiny pounds when we brought her home. She seemed incredibly small to us for a fourteen-week old puppy, but Dr. Ron assured us it was exactly where she should be for her age. She didn't weigh as much as Cooper's head. Even ill, she was full of energy. The big dogs did not intimidate her. In fact, she ran them in circles. We tried to introduce them one at a time, but Izzy would have none of that. She wanted to see them all at once. She jumped from Ray's protective arms to the floor, grabbed one of Cooper's toys and ran, Madison, Cooper and Morgan in pursuit. Gus didn't have the energy to chase her, but he watched with immense curiosity. Cooper grabbed his toy and with Izzy still holding on, carried it back to the family room. He lay down on his bed on top of his toy and Izzy curled up beside him and went to sleep. They became inseparable.

My Dad came to visit shortly after we brought Izzy home. I was beginning my radiation treatment and frankly felt less then chipper. Dad adores dogs, so Izzy was under his guidance for two weeks. He taught her the Invisible Fence boundaries, how to use her dog door and gave her some basic obedience training and potty training. He essentially took her off my hands, for which I was grateful. Trying to housebreak her was an enormous challenge. In return, Izzy's sharp puppy teeth punctured my dad's fragile skin so many times that he looked like he had fought a battle with an alligator. He was covered in Band-Aids.

Izzy 2007 –

Two years old with a patched up Horton,

who you will read about shortly...

Have Dog, Will Travel

Months passed, I was through the worst of my cancer treatment. My business was for sale and I was presented with an offer I could not refuse. About the same time, Ray's company asked him to extend his contract for another five years. We had already purchased our retirement home in Florida and he had no interest in working much longer but the Board of Directors was persuasive. He gave it a great deal of thought and finally conceded to extend his contract only if the company would provide our housing in San Francisco; he did not want to commute from Portland for another five years and we certainly did not need to own three homes. The housing market was rough and selling our Portland home could take some time. His Board of Directors generously provided us a housing allowance. I made a three-day trip to the Bay Area finding the perfect home for us to rent that would allow our dogs. Luck was on our side. A home with acreage on

Belvedere Island; how lucky could we get? Lots of yard space, tons of privacy, paths through the woods and a great deck overlooking San Francisco Bay. We even had a view of the Golden Gate Bridge. "The dogs would love it," I thought, and Ray would be delighted. It was an authentic Mid-Century Modern home, a perfect setting for our furniture and a fitting home for the CEO of a Mid-Century Modern furniture company.

After twelve years in Portland, moving day was approaching quickly. The designated day for the closing on the sale of my business was also near. I was in my office preparing documents for the closing and making sure I had everything we would need. We had one final meeting with the purchaser the following day and I was hurrying perhaps more than I should have been. I had Izzy with me, tethered with the same twenty-five foot cable I had used for Morgan. Izzy had somehow wrapped her tether around the base of my chair and my right ankle. I jumped up to grab a document off of the printer. It was too late.

I was already off balance from chemo. I went down with full force on my left leg, snapping my ankle in many, many pieces. It was a spiral fracture. Lying prone on the floor, after letting out a few choice words, I was quieted by Izzy licking my face as if to say, "Sorry mom, I love you and I'm really, really sorry. Can we play ball?" The ambulance came and a co-worker took Izzy home. I went to the hospital and was prepared for surgery. One eight-inch plate, six screws, two pins and a cast later, I was ready to go home. It would not be the last time we said "ohhhhh, Izzy..."

That same month Gus started to go downhill rapidly. It had been coming for a while and at fifteen, it was time to let him go. Dr. Ron said he would not be strong enough to make the move with us to San Francisco. He slept beside my bed on his last night. His breathing was labored. He was tired and my injury had added more distress. He had a good life with us. He was loyal, loving and the best guardian anyone could ask for. Euthanizing him was such a hard decision for us and I think he was telling us it was okay and he was ready. His demeanor changed, he acted depressed. Just standing up after a nap was an enormous challenge for him. He was tired.

We sat in Dr. Ron's Comfort Room, a wonderful room with a sofa, comfortable chairs and soft lighting. Ray sat on the sofa with Gus in his lap. We held him, kissed him and told him how lucky he was that he was going to get to see Kashi, Lexington and Sutton again and they would introduce him to Turbo. He would also get to see his best dog buddies; North, a friend's golden retriever who had died from lymphoma just a month earlier and Charlie, a boxer he had been walking buddies with years earlier who had an unfortunate tangle with a truck. He looked up at us with those big brown eyes that said, "thank you for loving me," and he was gone. I had a dream about Gus that night and imagined him playing in a field of tennis balls with all of his buddies around him.

Cooper the Protector

The move to San Francisco was a three-ring circus. Ray had his hands full. In one day we had to go to my last chemo infusion, meet the lawyer at noon to finalize the closing of the sale of my business, take the new owners to each of the shops to introduce the managers, all while the movers loaded the moving trucks. By 8:00 PM we were ready to hit the road. With me in a wheelchair feeling the effect of Percocet and four dogs, Ray was not chancing an overnight stop. We drove straight through to San Francisco, stopping only once for gas. The dogs behaved perfectly. What Road Warriors!

Once again, The Invisible Fence Company installed a system ahead of time in the new house. When we arrived, the dogs needed to be shown the boundaries of their new yard just once and they were good to go. Thank goodness, because I was useless that day. All I could do was roll around in my wheelchair and check things off the inventory list. The dogs thought their new house was awesome. Izzy had been with me on my three-day trip to find the house, so she already knew the layout. She was in charge of introducing the rest of the gang to their new digs. They investigated the woods, ran up and down the hills to the old pond and generally supervised the delivery men. The house was on several levels, each with a deck. The dogs would race from the front door to the lowest guest level, enter from that deck, dash up the main stairway to the first level, run out through the living room deck and back in from the kitchen deck, out the front door and start all over. It never took them long to figure out a new game and this house was like Disneyland for dogs!

We had deer, lots and lots of deer. The owner of our home installed an electric fence to keep them out and it worked fairly well until the power went out or the deer were too tempted by the lush landscaping and vegetable garden. The deer seemed to know exactly when the electric fence was not working. One morning I opened the front door to let the dogs out for their morning run. Cooper was right beside me. As I opened the door, I was greeted by the nose of an eight-point buck standing no more than a foot from the door, chomping on some greenery. Cooper turned himself inside out. Woo Woo Boy was terrified and never used that door again without peeking around the corner first and checking for monsters.

Izzy liked to chase the birds. She would perch herself on our middle deck and wait for a bird to fly by, then launch herself off the back of the bench seat. Her challenge was that the landing strip was twenty feet below the deck. She made it every time, all bones intact but it never failed to take my breath away.

The San Francisco Bay is home to many large birds, including Sea Eagles. To them, Izzy probably looked like a nice rabbit-sized meal. Cooper was Izzy's protector, always with an eye to the sky. When he saw the large birds circling he would bark and herd Izzy into the house or to the safety of his legs. They were a good team and best friends. He tried his best to keep her out of trouble and guard her.

I think Cooper's protection instincts were what started his dislike of our landlord. "Mohawk" was how we referred to him, because even though he was a wealthy sixty year old man, he did indeed have a Mohawk hairstyle. He had a difficult time understanding the difference between homeowner and landlord, often treating us as though we were unwanted houseguests. He was working on restoring some areas of the home and was always around. There was a small out-building on the back of the property where he was laying marble floors and remodeling the cabin-like bedroom into a true guest cottage. Mohawk was a unique character and we suspected he could even be living in this little cabin. Power lines and cable TV lines suddenly appeared, hijacked from the main house to the cottage.

He walked into our home unannounced very early one morning, while I was still asleep in bed. He came into the bedroom and said, "good morning, sunshine." Cooper launched at him, jumping from the bed to the door in a single leap. He was not going to let an intruder hurt his family. Soon after, our washing machine failed and a new one was ordered. On installation day, we were away and although we had told him not to come into the house, Mohawk let himself in to install the new washer. Cooper must have been quite unhappy about it and when we arrived home found Cooper with an enormous black eye and white caulking on his head, a caulking gun still sitting on the kitchen table. We could only guess what had happened. We could not risk any further injuries to Cooper and had to ask for a restraining order against Mohawk, banning him from his own property and forcing him to hire a property manager. Cooper had very good instincts when it came to protecting his family.

Because Izzy was raised with much larger dogs, she never learned to play gently. She happily threw her nineteen pounds up against Madison's sixty pounds, Cooper's hundred-ten pounds and Morgan's whopping hundred-sixty-five pounds. In her tiny little head she needed to be tough to survive. The big dogs would have been much happier if she toned down her tenacity a bit.

During an afternoon of hard dog play I heard a yip from Morgan followed by a fading scream from Izzy. Izzy had nipped Morgan on the ear and Morgan shook her head to throw Izzy away from her, as Lexington had done with Madison years earlier. Izzy went flying. This time there was no wall to stop her, only a forty-five foot drop down a very steep hill. I raced down the hill to where she had landed.

She was not moving. Then I saw her eyes open and she cried. She had broken ribs, a concussion and a pneumothorax. She was bleeding badly and having difficulty breathing. I gently picked her up not wanting to cause further damage, wrapped her tightly in a towel to keep her still, grabbed my car keys and raced to the vet. I dialed the vet on my cell phone, then called Ray, all while holding Izzy on my lap and driving sixty miles an hour in my little red Mini Cooper. She whimpered non-stop, a pathetic, "mommy help me" whimper.

Her breathing was labored. The vet tech was waiting for me in the parking lot and whisked her away. Ray met me in the lobby and we waited in stunned silence for what seemed like hours. Finally Dr. Susan came out and told us Izzy would be okay. Izzy would have died if I hadn't been there to see what had happened. Playtime would now need to be monitored much more closely. We were hoping Izzy would learn to calm down.

That was wishful thinking.

HELLLOOOO!!!!

Just before Christmas we were shopping and noticed a stuffed elephant at Macy's, a Talking Horton from Dr. Seuss's <u>Horton Hears A Who</u>. "Cooper would love that!" Ray said excitedly. We bought the elephant and it instantly became his favorite toy. He carried Horton everywhere and learned how to make him talk by hitting the correct spot on his front leg.

"Helllllooooooo"

and

"I said what I meant and I meant what I said, an elephant's faithful one hundred percent".

Izzy would steal Horton and cause him bodily harm, usually pulling out some stuffing or chewing his trunk. I would patch him up and Cooper was satisfied, but I realized we should have a back up if Horton ever met with the jaws of death. Macy's only had three left in stock in the entire company. We bought them. Slowly Horton I was replaced by Horton II, III and

IV. We had to scour EBay to find more.

If Horton needed a bath, Cooper would watch with apprehension in his eyes as Horton was placed in the washing machine. He would sit and watch him through the glass door going round and round until the washer was done. He would watch again as he tumbled in the dryer and let me know when he was finished. When they were reunited, Cooper would always press on Horton's front leg to make sure he was all right.

As long as a resounding *"Helllloooo"* came out he was satisfied. Once, Horton stayed in the dryer too long causing some damage to his voice box. When Cooper punched his leg, the familiar words came out but at ten times the normal speed, as though Horton had inhaled a LOT of helium.

"Hellllooooooo." "I said what I meant and I meant what I said, an elephant's faithful one hundred percent." "Hellllooooooo." "I said what I meant and I meant what I said, an elephant's faithful one hundred percent." "Hellllooooooo." "I said what I meant and I meant what I said, an elephant's faithful one hundred percent."

I started laughing hysterically.

Cooper dropped Horton and began repeatedly punching his leg with his nose. The voice kept coming out very fast and very high pitched. The more he punched, the more I laughed until I was laughing so hard I started crying. Cooper was not amused.

When Horton needed a patch from a battle with Izzy, Cooper would sit as I sewed him up, watching with great concern. I always wondered if he remembered getting stitches and knew that needles hurt. Horton always got a nose nudge or two as if Cooper wanted to comfort him. He was so smart, quite sensitive and very kind.

Irene and Izzy

Toilet Water Always Tastes Better

Ray's mom Irene came to visit us at Christmas and it became quickly apparent that she could not return to her home in Rhode Island and live on her own anymore. Alzheimer's was setting in at a frightening pace. The thought of living with us and our houseful of rowdy dogs was not quite how she envisioned her life. She thought they were loud and called them the "Wild Indians." And the dirt...the dogs shed, they carried mud into the house on their feet, Cooper dropped food on the floor and ATE OFF THE TABLE and the worst violation of all...they drank out of the toilet!

We all had a lot of adapting to do and the dogs showed everyone how it was done. Every time she yelled at them, they walked up to her and gave her a kiss or nuzzled her hand. If she was in one of her moods, they knew to keep their distance.

They seemed to sense her inability to walk in a straight line and were careful around her. They slowed down when she was coming down the hall and sometimes even offered her their head to steady her when she was wobbly. They adapted.

We would often find her sitting in a chair patting a head or scratching an ear. She couldn't fool us. She was starting to enjoy their company. Ray and I both knew his dad was looking down on us and chuckling at the irony.

Irene liked Izzy the best. She was a reasonable size and liked to sit on Irene's lap. As puppies go, Izzy was usually pretty good. She never got into a lot of trouble. She chewed a few kitchen cabinet corners, but nothing that was irreparable. She ate her share of shoes, but that was our fault for leaving them on the floor. Pens were her failing. Bic pens, expensive fountain pens, hotel giveaway pens...they all got her into trouble. She would seek them out from the desk or Ray's pockets. If he hung his coat on the back of a chair when he came home from work, she would search the coat pockets for pens. He always did the crossword puzzle while riding the ferry to and from work so she knew there would most always be a pen in his pocket. If she got one, it was destroyed in a matter of seconds as well as any surface the ink bled onto. The beige carpet in the library and master bedroom had streaks of blue and red from ink we could never get fully cleaned.

Maria, our wonderful housekeeper, would work for hours on the stains trying to help us get them out. One evening Izzy had grabbed a red pen from my desk. It happened in a flash. She must have been scoping it out for some time. It took her a millisecond to jump up on the chair, grab the pen and take off through the house with me running after her screaming for her to stop. Thankfully the red ink blended well into the dark hardwood floors. For about a year, Izzy's pretty white fur around her mouth was stained red, blue and purple from the monumental amount of pen eating she did.

barbara boswell brunner

Izzy Walks On Water. Well, Sort Of...

Since Izzy could fit under an airplane seat, we started taking her with us on our trips to the Florida house. She would sit under the seat like an angel, falling asleep as soon as the door shut and waking up at wheels down. She was an amazing traveler, even earning her wings from United Airlines. One pilot remarked to me that she behaved better than most children. The flight attendants adored her and we often got the same flight crew. They always looked forward to greeting Izzy.

On our first trip with Izzy, we arrived in Florida late at night. It was wintertime and our caretaker had placed the floating solar blanket on the pool to keep the water warm. We opened the door to the pool deck and Izzy raced through the doorway. Before we could blink, Izzy was standing in the middle of the pool, on top of the now-sinking solar blanket. Ray and I both started yelling at her and of course just confused the heck out of her. She stopped, she went forward, she backed up toward us, all while the blanket continued to sink.

Choices rapidly chattered in our heads. As the cover sank it began to wrap into a cone-shaped envelope of death, now too far from the edge for us to grab. If we dove in after her, we took the risk of getting ourselves tangled. It was only seconds but it seemed like hours. With one great terrier leap, she managed to make it to the deck. Disaster averted. We could not sleep for hours from the adrenaline rush. On the same trip she managed to fall in backwards while not paying attention to her footing. As we now know, Izzy was going blind at a young age and likely did not see the pool well at night. By the age of four, she was ninety percent blind in one eye and fifty percent blind in the other. Ah yes...the poster still rules.

Izzy is still not fond of the pool, although we did teach her how to swim and where to get out if she ever falls in without us close at hand. Every couple of weeks we put her in the deep end and let her swim out. Izzy paddles to those stairs like an Olympian, a pissed off Olympian, but an Olympian nonetheless.

While we vacationed in Florida, the big dogs had a new sitter in San Francisco. The sitter's name was Jessica. She was the niece of someone who had worked with Ray for years and came with glowing references. On our first meeting to introduce her to the dogs, we were concerned. She couldn't have weighed more than ninety pounds, soaking wet. We wondered if she would be comfortable with three big dogs. Our concerns were quickly averted as she lay down on the floor with Morgan and Cooper. She was in heaven—Cooper had a new girlfriend! Of course, if I had known then that Jessica bungee jumped off of the bridge over Victoria Falls in South Africa that same year, I would not have worried quite as much.

Jessica loved all of the dogs, but she had a special fondness for Cooper. She was a budding photographer and loved to take photos of the dogs. They were fabulous photos. She would load new ones on my screen saver for me after each of our trips so we could enjoy them all of the time. There would be a photo of Cooper, then Madison, then Cooper, then Morgan, then Cooper, then Cooper again...he was her favorite subject and he loved to pose. He was quite the ham and so photogenic.

We forgot to tell Jessica about talking Horton. On her first night in the house she had all of the dogs piled into the bed with her and she was sleeping soundly. Suddenly..."*I said what I meant and I meant what I said, an elephant's faithful one hundred percent!*" rang out. Jessica jumped out of bed—who's in the room? Her heart was pounding as she noticed the dogs were all asleep. "Lousy guard dogs," she mumbled. Then, "*Helllloooo*" came from under the blankets. "Holy crap, the dogs talk in their sleep," she thought, as she shook herself awake. "Wait a minute...."The dogs can TALK"? Then she discovered Horton under the covers. Cooper had rolled over onto his "talker." With a sigh of relief she fell back into bed, snuggling with Cooper for the rest of the night.

In August 2010, our Florida vacation was cut short by a frantic call from Jessica. Morgan would not get out of bed. She tried everything including food bribes, but she would not move. If Morgan would not get out of bed for food, something was seriously wrong. Ray jumped on the next available plane. When he arrived home, Morgan was still in her bed. Jessica had done as much for her as she could, but Jessica was no match for Morgan's now incredible hundred-sixty-five pounds.

With the help of a friend, Ray was able to lift her with the sling we still had from her other surgeries and rushed her to Dr. Susan. The MRI showed Morgan had not only blown her right ACL as we had suspected, she also had a broken leg. Two days of holding her bladder caused a raging kidney infection. She was in bad shape. After five days of IV antibiotics and loving care from Dr. Susan, Morgan was ready for another surgery. Another titanium plate and several screws and pins later, Morgan was home, ready for her new TV role as the Six Million Dollar Dog.

Hmmm...wish that had worked out...

barbara boswell brunner

Pito + Cooper = FIRE!

Anytime we were not in the kitchen there was the possibility of Cooper counter surfing, as we found out one wintry evening. Cooper was notorious for stealing food from the counters or dinner table. His behavior was pathological and quite stealthy, running his nose along the counter to see where the choicest tidbits were located, and then with one quiet move, feet never touching the counter, the food would be abducted.

When we had large parties with food being served in various courses, we had to assign a table guard to keep Coops from emptying dinner plates before everyone was seated. Counter surfing, he stole a full pound of Spanish goat cheese along with a bowl of olives and made himself very, very sick. Extra precaution had to be taken during and after every meal to ensure everything was cleaned up and the counter was Cooper-proofed. We thought we finally had it under control...

Retiring to the library one evening, Cooper repeatedly came into the room and seemed more jittery than usual. He paced back to the hallway and turned around into the library again. Something seemed to be bothering him. Then we both smelled smoke. Since we had two wood burning fireplaces, we initially thought that a gust of wind had blown down the flue and stirred up some ash. Maybe that was what Cooper was trying to tell us? As we continued to smell smoke, an investigation seemed warranted.

As I approached the kitchen the smell became stronger. Flames were shooting from the cooktop. Our teapot, Pito by Frank Gehry, was sitting on top of the stove. Cooper must have been counter-surfing and accidentally turned on the gas burner under the teapot. It heated up to a pretty shade of crimson and caught the large wood handle on fire. The smoke we smelled was the handle burning. Normally this would not be so worrisome; a hard surface counter would stop any flames from spreading...except our counters were made of walnut. A few minutes more and the kitchen may have gone up in flames. Ray was hot on my heels, searching for the source of the smell. He, being braver than I, grabbed the flaming teapot, knowing we were seconds away from a disaster, and threw it into the sink. Cooper solemnly observed as we doused it with water; his big head peeking around the corner of the kitchen door with an expression of remorse, his eyes begging for forgiveness. We removed the knobs from the stove that night and put them back on only when we were cooking.

barbara boswell brunner

Remove Your Shoes...
Take Your Chances

Ray's job required us to do a lot of entertaining and it was more fun for us to cook at home than go out to a restaurant and much more fiscally responsible. The company was paying for our home and it just made sense to use it for entertaining the designers and other company visitors who were continuously coming into San Francisco for meetings. We had tons of bedrooms and often put up the overnight visitors.

Our home was the perfect platform for entertaining. Ray loved to cook and we had company dinners at the house several times a week. The dogs got used to seeing the constantly changing faces of employees and designers and enjoyed the entertaining as much as we did. Matt, Dow and Carol were our constants and they attended most every dinner party. They were all dog lovers and each had their favorite. Matt loved Cooper, Dow adored Izzy and Carol took on both Morgan and Madison. It would not be unusual to see ten or twelve people sitting around the table with Cooper's head resting beside Matt's plate and Morgan or Madison sitting on Carol's feet. The only well-behaved child around the table was Izzy. We started teaching her manners early and she never begged at the table. It's a shame her other lessons were not as well retained.

Izzy was a typical terrier trouble-maker; strong willed and tenacious. She had a penchant for stealing shoes and destroying them in seconds. Dow sat with her one evening after the guests had gone and took off his brand new shoes. Izzy took that as an open invitation and grabbed one and darted off to the woods, Dow and I in drunken pursuit. Izzy won. We never did find that shoe and Dow went home that evening in his socks.

Cooper was in food heaven in San Francisco. With the amount of entertaining we did, he always had plenty of food to taste, beg for and steal. We also had a very large vegetable garden where we grew tomatoes, artichokes, herbs of every variety, lemons, figs and persimmons. Cooper had a particular fondness for tomatoes and would pull them directly off the plants to eat. Not just any tomato, no, he had to check through all of the plants to find one that was perfectly ripe and pluck it before we could find it for dinner. He also had a fondness for butter lettuce and figs. I am sure he thought it was very cool that we had made a grazing garden just for him. We were thoughtful parents.

barbara boswell brunner

Destination Florida

Ray's company was sold, a contract dispute arose with the new owner, and Ray threw in the towel. My cancer had taught us that life was way too precious for us to deal with the nonsense. We made a decision to move to our Florida home fulltime. I am a seasoned moving organizer and was up for the challenge! In just ten days we scheduled the moving company, packed, had the moving truck loaded and we were on the road...four dogs, one mother-in-law with Alzheimer's, Ray and me in a Suburban.

Our five-day road trip was daunting to coordinate. We needed hotels with connecting rooms that would accept four dogs. All reservations were made in advance and that meant we had a schedule to keep. We'd never had this crew in the car for so long and had no idea how we would fare. Each dog had a bed and a place for a leash to tether them to the car; Madison in the far back, Morgan in the third row, Cooper beside my mother-in-law in the second row (no, no tether for mom, but don't judge me for occasionally wishing for a gag) and Izzy under my feet.

The rules were that NO ONE open a door without doing a tether check. We could not risk any of this gang getting loose. Cooper was our big concern. He did not handle change very well. When I had him in my shops as a puppy, he would bark at the mannequins when their outfits got changed. He was extremely aware of anything new. He was mildly freaked out during our move to San Francisco and we both worried about how he would handle five hotel rooms and another new house.

Feeding and walking four dogs on the road was challenging but they all handled it like champs—up at dawn, breakfast in the room, out for morning potty time. Izzy and Cooper walked together then got loaded and tethered in the car. Madison and Morgan walked together and then they got tethered. Ray stayed in the room and watched out for his mother who was very confused and having more trouble with the trip than the dogs. Our midday gas stop was potty trip number two for the day. While Ray pumped gas, I walked dogs. People at the gas stations looked at us like we were crazy getting all of the dogs out of the car. Ray's mom continually asked when we were going to arrive in California. By evening we were all ready to collapse into bed but first we needed doggie dinner and walks. By the time we pulled into the Florida driveway we were exhausted but had not had a single crisis on the road.

Izzy and Madison were both quite familiar with the Florida house and raced around happy to be out of the car. Morgan was fascinated by the pool and boats traveling up and down the waterway. Cooper was overwhelmed and buried himself in the bedroom. It took a few days, but once our furniture arrived from San Francisco they were getting settled in. They had a dog door, an Invisible Fence and a cool yard to race around in.

We prepared our neighbors for the dogs, especially warning about Cooper and his VWD. Every neighbor got the drill on letting us know if Cooper was injured in any way. This was the first time we had lived in a "neighborhood." The dogs were used to running free on acres of property, now we had a regular city-sized lot. We knew it would be a tough adjustment for all and we told each neighbor that we appreciated their patience as the dogs got adjusted. We were fortunate that our cul-de-sac was full of families with dogs. We had Beau, a quiet Shepherd mix; Harry, a handsome Wheaton Terrier; Lily, a crazy Yorkshire terrorist; Sophie, an itsy-bitsy

Chihuahua and Ben, an enormous Great Dane. There was also a Pit Bull that none of us knew the name of. He was kinda quiet and kept to himself...

It took some adjustment time for everyone but eventually they all got adjusted to each other. Cooper and Sophie had a love affair going on and would "talk" to each other on a regular basis. The Invisible Fence worked great, but we had a neighbor on one side that was a bit timid around dogs. Since our homes were close together and our dog door was on their side of our house, we also installed a hard fence, a nice simple four-foot tall picket style fence. The dogs quickly got used to the gardeners and the pool boy but never to those timid neighbors. Their hesitation around these neighbors was a cause of much barking over the next year, causing them to request we put a bark control collar on Cooper if he was to continue to use the dog run. As much as it pained us, we wanted to be good neighbors, and complied.

Doggy Paddlin' School

The dogs all needed to learn about water safety. We had a pool and were directly on the waterway. Their Invisible Fence would keep them away from the seawall, but the pool was available to all. One at a time we placed them in life vests, carried them, or in Morgan's case, strongly urged her into the water. The steps were wide and shallow flanking each end of the pool—designed by Ray specifically for the dogs' safety. We let them get used to the water a little at a time, finally scooping them up and floating with them. They all learned where the steps were and how to use them. We fit Madison and Izzy each with a Safety Turtle as an extra precaution. It is a wonderful device, invented to save small children from downing. It is in the shape of a turtle and fits to the wrist with a small plastic lock. We converted two of them for the dogs, attaching the device to each collar. If either Izzy or Madison fell into the pool by accident, an extremely loud alarm would ring in the house. Cooper took to the water immediately and we knew Morgan was a strong swimmer, as much of her physical therapy from surgery was done in a pool.

One afternoon I was outside getting some sun. Madison by now was quite old and getting feeble. She walked to the edge of the pool and just fell in. Perhaps her eyes were failing or maybe she had a stroke. Instead of doggy paddling to the edge or the stairs, she sank. She made no effort to save herself, no struggle, no flailing; just a quiet plop and she was out of sight. I dove in, pulling her back to the surface. She was limp. I held her upside down to shake out any inhaled water. She was still limp but her eyes were open and blinking. She was alive! Cat Life number nine. That evening Ray and I put a life vest on her and the three of us got into the pool. She just hung limply in the life vest. We tried moving her legs to show her how to paddle and she made no effort. She had forgotten how to swim. We knew her time with us was coming to an end.

Madison was failing, she was not eating well, sleeping most of the time and we knew it was time for us to let her go. She was fifteen years old and had lived a fabulous life. She got to travel, see new places and meet new people and new four-legged friends. We made an appointment with the vet. We sat on the floor with her for quite a long time, Madison lying on a fluffy warm blanket. A dose of Valium calmed her down. When we had finished our goodbyes she got the final shot and went quietly to sleep. She looked so peaceful and sweet. She even seemed to have a smile lingering on her face. I knew she was in Doggie Heaven pointing at our Most Wanted poster and smiling. She brought so much joy and lots of mischief into our lives. We were better people for it. Madison was the epitome of unconditional love. No matter how many times she was scolded she was always ready with a wagging tail and a kiss. She saw the silver lining in every bad situation. Madison was an optimist. Madison was loved.

barbara boswell brunner

No Tofu, Please

Morgan had ballooned in weight from the time we left Portland to arriving in Florida. She was now one hundred-sixty-five pounds. Dr. Greg insisted we put her on a diet and get at least twenty five pounds off as soon as possible. Morgan went from eating four cups of kibble a day to two. The unfairness of it, I am sure she thought. Cooper ate six cups of food a day and was skinny as a rail. Morgan was always hungry and always begging.

Our friends Dane and Ellen came to visit for a week from Portland, Oregon. They are both very serious vegetarians. We prepared for their visit by stocking the fridge with as many vegan friendly items as we could, including tofu sandwich meat. No...meat is too generous of a word—I'll call it sandwich filler.

We were preparing for a day at the beach and Ellen made a sandwich for Dane, wrapping it in plastic wrap and placing it in the center of the kitchen island. Surely that would be out of

Cooper's reach, Ellen thought to herself. While we were out of the room, Cooper apparently stretched to the center of the counter and stole the sandwich. After discovering the contents were not as gourmet as he would like, he dropped it on the floor. In seconds it was in Morgan's mouth AND being swallowed whole. The four of us were dumbfounded that she COULD swallow it whole; her mouth was like that of a shark, unhinging enough to swallow her prey.

We rushed Morgan to the Emergency Vet Clinic, where after an hour of induced vomiting she "heaved" up the sandwich, still intact in plastic wrap. The vet came into the room and told us Morgan was fine and would be brought up to us in a moment. She then asked, "What was that sandwich made from? I have to ask because it was so disgusting I want to make sure I NEVER eat it." We howled with laughter thinking Cooper with his gourmet tastes probably thought that, too.

My Anger Cannot Be Expressed In Words

We were just getting adjusted to the loss of Madison when another tragedy struck. I was working in the kitchen, where the dog door was located. I heard Cooper barking in the dog run fairly insistently and he was wearing his bark collar, so I knew something was terribly wrong. Before I had a chance to go outside and investigate I heard a yelp and seconds later Cooper came crashing through the dog door, followed by Izzy. He was whimpering and refused to go back out the door. Izzy looked terrified.

What in the world was going on, I thought. I walked out to their dog run and could not see anything that would have caused his yelp, only two men working on the air conditioner next door, just on the other side of our fence. I waved at them and they did not respond. It seemed odd.

After dinner that evening, Cooper and Izzy both refused to use the dog door and instead had to be walked to the backyard and let out the pool door, where there were three steps. Cooper had trouble navigating the stairs, walking like he was drunk and stumbled down the stairs. I was worried and called Dr. Greg and asked if I could bring Cooper in the next morning.

After an inconclusive examination and x-ray, Dr. Greg said he could not find anything wrong except for a little distortion on his lower spine. He said it would be possible at Cooper's age for him to be getting some disk compression in his spine. He did not feel it was anything worth worrying about and I brought Cooper home. He was groggy from the anesthesia, so we put him to bed. By midnight we realized there was indeed something very wrong. He could not stand up and had soiled himself in his bed. We cleaned him up, got him a fresh bed and I slept on the floor with him for the remainder of the night. He couldn't tell me what was wrong and I felt so helpless.

The next morning was Saturday and Dr. Greg was out of town but left a phone number if we needed him. I called and he instructed us to go immediately to the emergency clinic. I did not want to go alone and called my friend and neighbor Kim. She was in the middle of coloring her hair and yet did not hesitate for a second.

She rinsed, shoved her hair into a baseball cap and was at the house in less than two minutes. Ray was boat shopping with Kim's husband that morning. They were already located an hour and a half south. Kim and I wrapped towel slings around Cooper's stomach and chest and carried him to the car. After the clinic's initial exam and a phone consultation with Dr. Greg it was decided that we needed to go immediately to the veterinary specialists in Tampa, where there was a neurologist on staff. It was a two-hour drive, north.

Cooper lay on the back seat of my car, quiet and looking frightened. He soiled himself again. He didn't understand why he couldn't walk and neither did I. He had just been swimming with me. He loved to join me in the water when I did laps. All it took was "Cooper, go SWIM!" He had been so strong and healthy just forty-eight hours earlier. This did not make sense.

Arriving in Tampa, we were met by a most attentive veterinary staff. They hovered over Cooper immediately, gently carrying him out of the car and into the examination room. We discussed what some of the problems could be: a tumor, a slipped disk, an injury. I informed them that Cooper was Von Willebrand's Deficient. If he needed surgery they would need clotting factor. They added internal bleeding to the list of possible ailments. Cooper was taken into the back to be examined by the neurologist and Kim and I waited in the room. Kim tried her best to cheer me up. In the year that she had known him, Kim had come to love Cooper, too. This ailment was so sudden and unexpected. I was in shock.

The neurologist did not come back with good news after viewing the x-rays. Without an MRI he could not be sure, but his suspicion was that there was not much that could be done to save Cooper. A hundred pound dog with a spinal injury and needing spinal surgery would be difficult enough and his VWD made surgery more challenging. It is possible he would not even survive surgery. It was also possible the surgery would not help him and he would be permanently paralyzed. Even if the surgery was a success, it could take months for him to heal requiring two people to carry him everywhere.

When Cooper had first arrived, the neurologist tested for deep pain in his front and back legs and found no reaction in the back legs but did get a reaction from his front legs. An hour later when he tested for deep pain a second time, Cooper showed no reaction at all, even with full force of the forceps between his toes. He appeared to have no feeling at all from the neck down. This was inconsistent with the previous day's x-ray, which showed no damage or problem with his upper spine, just the lower spine.

The neurologist was stumped. He gave me the options and said the decision was up to me. He would do everything possible to save Cooper, but could not guarantee his survival. He left us alone to talk.

I called Ray, who offered to drive four hours to Tampa. I told him in my heart I did not believe Cooper had four hours to live. I didn't know if he was suffering, but I could not bear it if he were. Ray told me to do what I thought was best. After some deep soul-searching, Kim was able to help me work through the decision to euthanize Cooper. We hugged and cried. Having her with me to help make the decision was something I will never forget. Our friendship developed an impenetrable bond over this experience.

The techs moved us into a larger and more private room and placed Cooper on a blanket. I could tell by looking at his face that he was at peace. The fear was gone and he was calm. Kim and I sat on the floor with him, crying and hugging him. I called Ray and held the phone to Cooper's ear so he could say goodbye. Kim and I each held one of his big monster paws. I lay down on the blanket, hugged him with a full body hug and said goodbye. I held him tightly as he took his last breath. Kim and I barely spoke on the ride home fearing one of us would break down into a puddle of tears.

I took Horton to bed with me that night and hugged him all night long. Cooper would have liked that. Jessica, our San Francisco dog sitter was as devastated at the news of Cooper's passing as we were. She had always intended to visit us in Florida, but never had the time. Now her favorite boy was gone. Ray and I thought that Ellie the giant elephant needed a home. She was just too big for us to keep. Izzy would destroy her and we couldn't give her to Goodwill. Jessica had a new puppy. Olives still sleeps with Ellie every night and hopefully dreams happy dreams of Cooper.

I did not know it the day Cooper died, but one of the vet techs took a clay paw imprint from Cooper before he was sent for cremation. I received it in the mail a few weeks later and collapsed to the floor hugging it and bawling for an hour. What a sweet gesture. Any time I am feeling blue I like to hold it and rub my fingers on his toe imprints. Remembering what a special dog he was makes me smile again. I will always have a part of him with me.

The neurologist did an autopsy and found that Cooper had an injury to his spine that appeared to be some sort of blunt force trauma. Because of his VWD he slowly bled internally, causing the paralysis. Cooper bled to death. I was shocked and the image of the two men working on the air conditioner next door haunts me. Izzy saw what happened that fateful day and it frightened her so badly that she has never again used the dog door. She is not timid in any other area of her life. Her instincts are to attack first, think later, and then attack again. I wish she could tell us what happened to Cooper.

I miss having to hide food and guard the dining table. I miss his woo, woo, woo. I miss his night-time snuggles under the covers. I miss his quirkiness. I miss his knowing eyes and his kind spirit. Horton now sits on a shelf in my closet. I still occasionally press his leg to hear *"Helllooooo"* and it makes me smile.

Sometimes it seems as though things happen for a reason. We would have never been given the opportunity to have Cooper in our lives if cancer had not taken Lexington so suddenly. Cooper was a gift we will always treasure, a gift we came close to never having, whose life could have been cut short at seven weeks of age because he had blue eyes. I am alive today because of Cooper. We were blessed to have had his love. Our home resonates with emptiness.

Conclusions

Our friends have often thought us to be nuts. One huge dog, maybe... but we liked multiples. We never had less than two most of our married life and often had three, four, and for a while even five dogs at once. Our homes were always a chaotic, raucous circus filled with slobber, copious amounts of dog fur and most importantly, love. With all of its canine energy, our home has always been my personal Zen retreat. My work life was hectic. Although I was providing a Zen-like environment to my clients, actually producing that feeling was not at all peaceful or relaxing. Coming home after a long day of dealing with the drama of entrepreneurship, our dogs were my respite. Their chaos was my Zen. Being allowed to love them was the greatest peace of all. Oh, and an understanding cleaning lady was a handy addition!

To some, our home has always been a madhouse, full of chaos and drama. To me...not at all. Just walking through the front door at night and being greeted by a big sloppy puppy kiss made the worst of days seem okay. The unconditional love of a dog cures many ills.

Did we err in adopting Izzy? Did we fail in our parenting of her? I don't know that anyone has the ability to give a definitive answer. When I see her at night snuggled on Ray's pillow, her back pressing tightly against his neck, I know we did okay. She brings us great joy and she makes us laugh. She has the ability to tug on our heartstrings at the most appropriate moments. She has taught us that it is possible to adapt to severe physical challenges and still be ready to play. Would she be a happier dog with her sight and hearing? Possibly. Would we be happier?

Oh, dear God, think of the trouble she could get into...

###

Epilogue

Morgan and Izzy are still with us. Morgan's weight is now down to a svelte hundred and seven pounds and she looks fabulous. She runs, chases planes in the sky, and is very active on her bionic legs. She looks forward to her weekly visits to Irene's nursing home. She is a great comfort to many of the older folks who had dogs in their earlier days. She loves to visit the rooms and get head pats. Morgan has her old-folks fan club.

Morgan and Izzy are not friends; they do not even tolerate each other much. We never realized what a true referee Cooper had been. He was the sheriff, the peacekeeper, Izzy's friend and protector. He was her partner in crime and her backup when she was afraid. Izzy has tried to take over Cooper's role as leader of the pack, the new sheriff in town. Morgan scoffs at her. She is patient and wonderfully tolerant of Izzy and does her best not to hurt her.

When Morgan finally passes on I doubt that we will add another puppy to our family. Izzy is intolerant of other dogs and will be best as an "only dog."

With Izzy's nineteen pounds verses Morgan's hundred-seven pounds their battles never have a good outcome, making the muzzle trick from years past unusable. Izzy attacks Morgan relentlessly, biting her ears and neck. Izzy has no common sense— most Parson Russell Terriers do not—and in her tiny little head she thinks she can dominate Morgan. Since Cooper's passing, Izzy has had more trips to the emergency vet to get sewn up than I can count on both hands. Dr. Cynthia now cares for Izzy and has advised us to muzzle her full-time. Izzy has a pretty pink leather basket muzzle decorated with silver daisies that she must wear any time she and Morgan are in the same room. We call it her "Suicide Prevention Device" At least she looks cute and girly when she acts like Cujo...

She continues to attack Morgan, even when wearing the muzzle. Morgan will not retaliate. Now when Izzy attacks, Morgan grabs her by the back of the neck, as a mother dog would with a misbehaving pup and drops her at my feet as if to say, "YOU deal with it." She walks away in disgust.

"Izzy, Stop it!" "Izzy, Leave It!"

"Oh, Izzy...we love you."

ABOUT THE AUTHOR

Barbara grew up in Lancaster County, Pennsylvania with her parents, sister and always a dog, or two or three. Meeting her husband in Washington, DC, they continued together on a journey as self-proclaimed dog addicts. In the ensuing years, she founded three successful businesses in the Pacific Northwest. She and her husband currently live in Southwest Florida with two dogs and copious amounts of dog fur.

She can be contacted on her Facebook Fan Page

www.facebook.com/authorbarbaraboswellbrunner

or by visiting

www.DogmaThe Book.com

Made in the USA
Lexington, KY
29 October 2012